· SEBASTIAN FAULKS'S

Birdsong

A READER'S GUIDE

PAT WHEELER

CONTINUUM | NEW YORK | LONDON

2002

The Continuum International Publishing Group Inc
370 Lexington Avenue, New York, NY 10017

The Continuum International Publishing Group Ltd
The Tower Building, 11 York Road, London SE1 7NX

www.continuumbooks.com

Printed in the United States of America

Library of Congress Cataloging-in-Publication Data

Wheeler, Pat, 1950–
   Sebastian Faulks's Birdsong : a reader's guide / Pat Wheeler.
      p. cm. — (Continuum contemporaries)
   Includes bibliographical references.
   ISBN 0-8264-5323-6 (alk. paper)
   1. Faulks, Sebastian. Birdsong. 2. World War, 1914–1948—Literature
and the war. I. Title. II. Series.
   PR6056.A89 B57 2002
   823'.941—dc21
                                        2002000991

Sebastian Faulks's
Birdsong

CONTINUUM CONTEMPORARIES

Also available in this series

Forthcoming in this series:

Contents

A life, they say, may be considered a point of light which suddenly appears from nowhere, out of the blue. The point describes a luminous geometrical figure in space–time; and then just as suddenly disappears. (Interesting to have seen the lights disappearing in Space–Time during one of the big battles — Death dowses the glims.)

Richard Aldington, 'Prologue", *Death of a Hero*.

Dedication

For David and Benjamin and Emily.

And for Sharon, Nahem, Sally, Sharon Wilson and Marilyn, wonderful friends who kept me sane during a difficult time and with special thanks to the nurses and doctors at Barnet Hospital Breast Unit and the doctors and radiographers at Middlesex Hospital Meyerstein Institute of Oncology for their fantastic care and support.

1

The Novelist

Sebastian Charles Faulks was born in Newbury, Berkshire in 1953. His father, Peter, was a solicitor who later became a judge and his mother, Pamela, was a saleswoman before she became a full-time housewife. Both parents played a role in World War II where his father was in the armed forces and his mother worked as a radar screen operator, tracking German bomber planes over Norway. His background is typically Home Counties, public school, and upper-middle class. In an interview with Tim de Lisle in the *Sunday Telegraph Magazine*, Faulks describes his parents as "straightforward, conventional and incredibly nice," but elsewhere he describes them as "stifled, wooden and emotionally repressed." The paradoxical nature of these statements reflects Faulks's double-edged vision on life in general and in many ways it has resonance in his writing. Faulks the man and Faulks the novelist embody a collection of contradictions.

Faulks was sent away to prep school at the age of eight and he was ostensibly happy there; he was, it seems, very good at both games and his schoolwork. After leaving his prep school he went on to be educated at Wellington College where from the age of fourteen or fifteen he contributed regularly to his school magazine. Faulks left Wellington to go to Emmanuel College, Cambridge to read English. In reality, this ostensibly happy and effortless childhood conceals a much darker and more problematic aspect to Faulks's early years. He led a quiet, ordered existence and he was only close to one person, his older brother Edward. He had few friends of his own and lived an almost cloistered life; he did not really socialize with anyone else until he was around fifteen years of age. According to de Lisle, Faulks the sporty child was also sickly, suffering from a range of complaints including asthma, hay fever, eczema, and a bad chest. He was not happy at Wellington either; his brother Edward claims that Faulks was "a sensitive boy in an insensitive school." Faulks describes it as having "the ethos of cold showers, cross-country runs and not standing out from the crowd." Boys were expected to blend in with the rest of the school, to become part of a unit and to be "disciplined, reshaped and corrected." It is apparent that Faulks's experience of all-male communities and the discipline inflicted upon him at school has had a profound effect on his writing. There is an irresistible impulse towards these modes of behavior in Faulks's portrayal of a certain type of "Britishness."

Faulks appears to have two irreconcilable parts to his character. He is a rebel who, in his own words, "demanded more drugs and women" while at school, yet he stayed on an extra year to gain more A levels so that he could go to Cambridge to study English. Faulks claims he was a "troubled soul" and had periods of great unhappiness in his adolescent years when he spent a lot of his time listening to pop music, drinking and smoking too much and doing too little work. Faulks admits to listening to pop music all day, everyday, whether he was "drunk, sober or stoned." One day he realized that it was all "complete shit" and he claims he never listened to pop music again. However, it was during this traumatic and rebellious period that he started to write and the years he spent listening to pop music were not entirely wasted: while he was at Cambridge he wrote music reviews for student magazines. Faulks's main memories of Cambridge appear to be of those of wasted opportunity. He claims he did not work very hard, nor take his studies that seriously, which he now sees as a source of regret. However, in an interview for *Varsity* Faulks also recalls that while he was there he met people for whom literature was "the most important thing in the world." It was the first time he had met people who had a similarly serious view of literature to him and he found that incredibly inspiring. Faulks eventually graduated from Emmanuel in 1974 filled with determination to become a novelist. He took a Second, which he claims was "remarkable," considering he can only remember attending four lectures in two years.[1]

After leaving Cambridge, Faulks initially took a job teaching at a school in London and began to write freelance articles, mostly book reviews, for various papers. In 1978 he left teaching to take a job as a reporter with the *Daily Telegraph* in London. By this time he was also running a book club, the New Fiction Society, but he still continued to write fiction. He became a feature writer on the *Sunday Telegraph* and in 1986 he was recruited by the *Independent* as its Literary Editor. He was later appointed as Deputy Editor of the *Independent on Sunday*. In his time as a journalist Faulks also contributed to the *Sunday Times*, the *Spectator*, the *Good Books Guide*, the *Literary Review*, and *Books and Bookmen*. He additionally wrote a fortnightly column for the *Guardian*. In 1991 he gave up full-time journalism to concentrate on writing his novels. Faulks claims he was very happy to leave and that he took voluntary redundancy because "he hated it." He does not really have a high opinion of journalists either, claiming that they get everything wrong, "all the time; everything is just slightly wrong." Realistically and somewhat ironically, he also notes that if he could no longer make a living from writing he would probably go back to work for a newspaper. Faulks still writes journalistic articles from time to time but he obviously prefers writing fiction. The reason he writes novels he says is because he is excited by ideas and because "reading has given me intense pleasure, and I feel a kind a drive to create things on paper."

Faulks met his wife, Veronica, when he was Literary Editor of the *Independent* and she worked for him as a reader. They married some time later and after spells of living and working in France, they now live in London with their three children. Faulks claims that being a father fulfills him in many ways and says that domesticity suits him. He frequently quotes one of his favorite authors to emphasize the point: "Flaubert said, the more tranquil the domestic life, the more the imagination can run free. I subscribe to that completely." He is seen as a "modern" man in that he is in touch with his feelings, he writes sympathetically and knowingly about women and he is not afraid to expose the emotional and vulnerable side of his character. In "Wot I Wrote" he confesses:

I was, on many occasions, completely overcome while writing, and there were about 12 scenes (in *Birdsong*) when I couldn't go on, and I just had to stop and go out in the garden. There is a 60 page description of the night before the Battle of the Somme, and that was the most difficult to write, because I knew what was about to happen . . . I had to break off maybe four, five or six times . . . I was shaking from head to foot with a mixture of anger and grief, rage and pity. That surprised me; one thinks of compassion as being a fairly downbeat emotion, I had no idea it could be such a raging emotion.

Despite this emotional response to his subject matter Faulks retains a slight "old school" persona and is often described as a quintessential Englishman. Tim de Lisle says that he has "the sort of assurance that can only be acquired at a public school" and despite being seen as somewhat diffident and assured, it is often commented upon that he has an edginess about him that is revealing. To many, Faulks is a writer whose work seems to be at odds with his character and there are a number of telling responses to Faulks the writer and Faulks the man. He often comments that people who know him are rather surprised there are no jokes in his novels and that all his writing is "serious." Others who have interviewed him call him quiet, reticent, tense, or even a bit tetchy and he is, according to his editor, "an intensely private man." In fact, Faulks appears to be all of these things; he is a complex and contradictory person and something of an enigma. He unselfconsciously writes of subjects that would remain unspoken in his own upbringing, he is happy to proclaim he is in touch with his "feminine" side, but, he is clearly not always at ease in disclosing the "real" Sebastian Faulks in interviews. He appears to be at odds with himself; from one viewpoint he seems to be in flight from the rigidity and oppression of his own upbringing and from another he seems to embrace all of the traditional and "old-fashioned" ideological views that were forced upon him as a child and adolescent. Faulks also comes across as a rather superstitious person. He still apparently writes his novels on the old manual, portable typewriter on which he wrote *Birdsong*. It is, he acknowledges, a very inefficient way of doing things, but he is happy with it. It is conceivable that the contradictions that are an intrinsic part of his character are indicative of both the range and scope of his writing and the tensions that are inherent within it.

BACKGROUND TO THE NOVEL

In 1988, Faulks went to France with a party of veterans to report on the 70th anniversary of the Armistice. The trip was organized by the historian Lyn Macdonald, whose books *Somme, 1914* and *They Called it Passchendaele* offer first hand accounts of the war together with its historical and political context. Macdonald first collected together a number of stories and reminiscences of World War I in the 1970s when she became acutely aware that most veterans were now very old men and there was a chance they would die without ever having told their stories. Although she had been before, it was Faulks's first visit to the battlefields and it proved to be something of a catalyst for his writing. He realized the man standing next to him had stood on the same spot over seventy years before and could describe to him exactly what it had been like to live and fight in the trenches. Faulks recognized that if it was within this man's memory it must be part of his own memory too, and he offers this event as a defining psychological moment in his feeling of connectedness to World War I. Although it is easily discernible that the history of the war and the memory of the men who fought in it are the main inspiration for *Birdsong*, it is France (the country and its people) that is also a source of stimulus for Faulks. For him, it is a place that resonates with "the presence of the past" and it is the past that is a cognitive factor in much of his writing. It is clear that his feelings about the country lend his writing a great strength and a beautifully realized sense of place not just in *Birdsong*, but also in the novels that make up the French trilogy, *The Girl at the Lion d'Or* and *Charlotte Gray*.

Faulks's starting point for *Birdsong* was a belief that the scale of World War I was "almost beyond human comprehension." He had seen Lutyens' war monument at Thiepval and was profoundly affected by it, not least by its astonishing size but also by the fact that every part of the monument was covered with names of thousands of young men who were missing and never found, either during or after the war. In the face of such overwhelming evidence of horror, Faulks felt it somewhat presumptuous to attempt to write the story of these men and was at a loss as to how he could recapture or recreate the conditions and feelings of the war. Two things happened that helped him; the first was the discovery of the extent of the mining operations in no man's land and the second was the discovery of a shell on the Somme battlefields he had taken to visiting. The shell somehow made him feel connected to the past and the life of the men in the trenches. The miners seemed to him to be living in "a kind of concentrated hell," separate from yet contained within "the greater inferno" of the war. This was a chance for Faulks to offer a new story of the war, a story that was virtually unknown and one that gave new insight into the terrible conditions of the war.

Faulks still felt the novel he wanted to write was beyond his reach and not within his grasp as a writer. He could not find a "way in" and he was extremely frustrated by this, but he eventually laid the foundations of the novel on a boating trip on the canals in the backwaters of the River Somme. During the trip he noticed that the sides of the canal were shuttered with wooden planks, as were the trenches on the Western Front and he saw piles of rotting vegetation on the sides of the canals and experienced an almost nauseous reaction to the stultifying atmosphere around him. The rotting vegetation made him think of the death and putrefaction of the trenches. He imagined a similar boat trip on the canal in a period before the war, when the Somme was just a river where families fished and went on trips and knew that this was where he would set the first part of his story. This was his "way in" and he knew that the events of the first part of the story would foreshadow the events of the second part, and that his main protagonist would be tested to the limits of his emotions in both parts of the story. By the time Faulks had completed his boat trip and walked back through Amiens the plot of *Birdsong* was clear in his mind. He eventually worked on the novel for over six months and during this time he was totally focused on his subject matter, dreaming constantly that he was in a dug-out in the Front line of a trench. He says it was not a particularly traumatic dream, unlike the soldiers who fought in the war who suffered years of dreams and hallucinations "I wasn't going over the top, we weren't being shelled. It was simply where I lived." In an act of faith and a further indication of Faulks's superstitious nature he collected a jar of earth from the Front Line and kept it on his desk throughout the writing of *Birdsong* in the hope it would "keep [his] hand steady."

Faulks is clearly preoccupied with war and the psychological damage that can result from war, but this is not surprising given his own background. When he was at school he recalls that he was aware, at a very early age, that his history master did not seem to have the words to describe World War I. He also remembers reading out the names of the boys who had given their lives in both World Wars at the school remembrance service and witnessed first hand the emotional response of his headmaster to the dreadful losses. He recalls having a sore throat at the end of the list and this caused him to wonder how so many people, from such a small school, could have died. He says these memories were stored in the back of his mind, as if subconsciously he knew that one day he would try to make sense of it all. Faulks also believed for a long time that he, like his father and grandfather, would fight in a war. He asserts:

Our grandfathers fought in one war, our fathers in a second and I certainly believed that I would fight in a third. It wasn't until I was 36 or 37 that I finally accepted there wasn't going to be a third world war. There is always a felling that my generation has got away with it and that we are the lucky ones who somehow escaped.[2]

Perhaps he attempts to explore the innermost psyches of the men in the trenches because he knows he will not now have to experience the horror of war for himself. Faulks is obviously intrigued by the question of how far is it possible to go in human experience and remain human. In order to debate this question Faulks decided to structure the book in three time scales, one before the war, one during the war, and one in the contemporary period. In all three sections the nature of human experience is shown, but in relation to the uses of the human body. It is important that the horrors of war are preceded by the love story with its focus on the sexual body, rather than the compromised bodies of men in wartime. He makes the point that during war, men's bodies are maimed, killed and dismembered, but in the other sections he shows they are also capable of expressing love, passion, and sexual arousal.

According to Faulks he did not intend the book to end in the way it does. As one of the key themes of *Birdsong* is the loss of sons, Faulks saw the birth of a son as a good way to end. It is also important to him that the book ends on a rising note. The modern sections are not so powerfully realized as the other sections of the novel and this is something of which Faulks is acutely aware. He claims that part of the reason for writing the modern sections is that they provide a way in to the modern reader. They throw into relief the horrors of the war section and they offer a commentary on contemporary life that shows why these distant, horrific events matter in our lives. Faulks feels that we do not fully realize the horror of World War I from our distanced perspective and he wanted *Birdsong* to move, challenge, and make readers think about the war. He creates a world that is separate from anything the reader knows, that they can inhabit for a while and experience the horrific lives of the soldiers on the Western Front. It is mainly young people who died in their thousands, a whole generation of men either lost or irrevocably damaged, and it is this that makes the history of the war so poignant. The novel is assiduously researched and the pity and the horror of war are presented with care and persistence through the different narrative strands. *Birdsong* is Faulks's attempt to "re-populate the fields" where so many thousands of young men were killed or maimed.

OTHER WORK

Faulks's first novel, *A Trick of Light*, was published in 1984, his second novel, *The Girl at the Lion d'Or*, was published in 1988. This was followed in 1992 by his third novel, *A Fool's Alphabet*, and in 1993 he published *Birdsong* to huge critical acclaim. Since then he has published *The Fatal Englishman: Three Short Lives* (1996), *The Last Enemy* (with Richard Hillary, 1997) the *Vintage Book of War Stories*, editor (with Jorg Hensgen, 1998), *Charlotte Gray* (1999), and *On Green Dolphin Street* (2001). *A Fool's Alphabet* is an experimental novel that follows a young man's life over twenty-six chapters, from A- Z, revealing a different fragment of his story. The chapters follow alphabetically and place names that are important in the character's life. *The Girl at the Lion d'Or* is a romantic novel set in France between World War I and II that received wide critical acclaim. It has at its center an intense love affair between Anne Louvet, a hotel waitress whose life is devastated when her family is destroyed in World War I, and Charles Hartmann, a recently married lawyer to whom she turns for help. Like Stephen in *Birdsong*, Charles Hartmann finds himself in the grip of powerful emotions that he cannot control. The book draws upon the uneasy situation in France in the years leading up to World War II and the tale of morality that the love story embodies reflects on both the characters and the country alike. *Birdsong, The Girl at the Lion D'Or*, and *Charlotte Gray* are all linked through location and history and there are certain characters that appear in more than one of the novels. Hartmann, for example, appears in *The Girl at the Lion d'Or* and *Birdsong*, while Levi appears in *Birdsong* and *Charlotte Gray*. All three novels are also closely related in theme and subject matter and are seen as a trilogy: they are all set against the background of war and all graphically depict the personal lives of the characters and the intensity of life during war, or in the aftermath of war. According to Faulks, *Charlotte Gray* is about a generation that "threw away its youth to protect the free world against the Nazis." He sees this generation as completely different to the previous one in its approach to war, and he shows that the men and women who fought were completely free from illusion about the war. *Charlotte Gray* is acclaimed for its "realisation of a complete female character" and it is certainly true that in the character of Charlotte Gray, Faulks creates a strong and innovative female to represent what he calls a "resourceful and determined generation." Faulks's novels frequently have leading female characters and he is often commended for this fact. However, not everyone is happy with his representation of women and many (female) critics feel that he aspires to reach a part of experience that he cannot necessarily know. Faulks counteracts this criticism and says that his female characters "have the texture of female experience" but only through the textual world he creates in his novels.

The three novels in the French trilogy are closely linked not only in their realization of strong female characters, but also by the main protagonists' attempts to transcend the limits of their existence. Faulks carries this theme into his next book, *The Fatal Englishman: Three Short Lives.* Whereas *Birdsong* is mainly the story of one man's life and the physical and emotional responses to war, *The Fatal Englishman* is a biography of three young men, Christopher (Kit) Wood, Richard Hillary, and Jeremy Wolfenden, who all died either by taking their own lives or in mysterious circumstances. Woods was a promising artist who died by jumping under a train just before his first major exhibition; Hillary was a well-known Battle of Britain pilot whose hands were badly damaged during a crash, but who eventually flew again and died in a mysterious night flight; and Wolfenden who was a foreign correspondent for the *Telegraph* in Moscow and whose death is also unexplained. Faulks engages with the brief lives of these men who are driven by despair and failure in many ways. Wood was apparently addicted to opium and was bisexual, Wolfenden was a brilliant scholar, but was an alcoholic and a homosexual, and Hillary, who wrote the bestselling memoir *The Last Hero*, underwent agonizing reconstructive surgery on his damaged hands.[3] All three men, however, went against societal expectations and rebelled against the conventions enforced upon them. For Faulks, the fact that they all died in mostly tragic circumstances makes their lives even more poignant.

In *The Vintage Book of War Stories* (co-edited with Jorg Hensgen), Faulks writes "I was the first male member of my family for more than 100 years who, when confronted by a German of the same generation, has at least not tried to kill him." In an act of rapprochement, Faulks and Hensgen bring together a selection of fictional writing about war in the twentieth century from World War I through to the Vietnam War. It includes stories of both soldiers and civilians that engage with Faulks's preoccupation with love, death, friendship, and endurance. The anthology contains excerpts from such diverse writers as Ernest Hemmingway, Siegfried Sassoon, Heinrich Boll, Kurt Vonnegut, and Italo Calvino, to the more contemporary writers such as James Salter, Pat Barker, John Fowles, and Tim O'Brien. In *On Green Dolphin Street*, Faulks's latest novel, he once again draws upon the presence of the past and the impact of war upon his characters; Frank and Charlie, both ex-servicemen, are deeply affected by their experiences during World War II. Mary, another well-drawn female character, is the wife of Charlie and lover of Frank and is deeply effected by a love affair. Faulks sets their stories against the wider context of the Cold War and the novel evokes well the menacing and threatening climate of fear that predominated during the McCarthy era of the late 1950s. The historical background he draws upon moves between the United States and Russia and also follows the Richard Nixon/ John F. Kennedy presidential elections. Faulks renders the closed and secret society of the Cold War era very skillfully and his characters are forced to operate under extreme duress and stress and on the very edges of experience. In all his work, Faulks attempts to define the limits of human endeavor against an historical past that has influenced the way we live now. He merges the private and the public in a forthright but engaging interrogation of the human experience.

2

The Novel

Birdsong is a novel that revisits both the history of World War I and the literary canon of World War I writing to "pick up the threads of the past" and to connect them with the present. Faulks's prevailing preoccupation in much of his writing is with the human condition and Birdsong is no exception. The novel's major themes are those of human endeavor and endurance in times of great adversity and in the face of overwhelming emotion. In the novel Faulks asks under what circumstances is it possible to still believe that life is tolerable and worth living. He tries to make some sense out of the awful pity of the war, not just for himself, but for others who may not know the full horror. Faulks uses the motif of love to debate the complexities of the human condition and to explore the many differing and often conflicting facets of personal behavior. It is love, in its many forms, that allows the reflection of the intense experiences he wishes to foreground, and in many ways the novel is an expression of Faulks's "love" for the men who endured the terrible realities of World War I. He says "the lives of those who die young are often more sensitive indicators of the pressure of public attitudes than lives lived long and crowned with honours," and the novel makes obvious how the lives of those who die young are shaped by "large impersonal events only later termed historical" that are generally beyond their control.[4] *Birdsong* is the result of what he calls an "intellectual decision" to write about those lives affected by war.

Birdsong is very simply a love story set in France against the backdrop of World War I. It is the story of a young man's attempt to make sense of the horror and abjection he sees all around him and his search for meaning among the desecration of war. The novel introduces its contemporary readership to the past through history and memory and to a future that is already known. It is preoccupied with profound and meaningful literary themes, such as those of human endeavor, heroism, and love. In engaging with such significant and momentous themes, Faulks is often compared to some of the great naturalist and realist writers of the late nineteenth and early twentieth centuries such as Flaubert, Proust, and Zola. Interestingly, he lists these writers as among his own literary influences and clearly his own writing embraces those literary traditions he values. His writing is frequently compared to that of Flaubert and Balzac, while his narrative style is said to reflect "Proustian-like cogitations." He is, however, more specifically a romantic writer who deals almost exclusively with the emotions of love, loss, and mourning and who is concerned with the "remembrance of things past." Faulks clearly believes that remembrance is prompted by emotion, but he also thinks that too much emotion can be self-indulgent. He argues that "if the lamentation of the dead is to be turned into something purposeful, it takes not just compassion, but will and judgement." He says that:

[W]hat took place on the banks of the river Ancre on July 1, 1916 when 60,000 British casualties were sustained in a single day; what took place at Arras and Passchendaele; the ripping up and evisceration of a country's youth, the fragmentation of its society; the grief of mothers, lovers and fathers, not some amorphous national sadness, but each pain, singly, multiplied . . . this more than anything else has shaped the century.[5]

He obviously believes that the terrible scale of World War I is something that has not been properly understood by people of his generation. In "Back to the Front with Tommy," Faulks recalls his visit to the killing fields of World War I and of being "initially repelled and bored" by it. For him, the war seemed "unmanageably remote" and the language he uses emphasizes his feelings of estrangement: "removed," "distant," "forgotten," "silence," and "mystery". Faulks surmises that the men who fought at the Somme and Passchendaele, those who had witnessed obliteration and extermination on such a monumental and unprecedented scale, were to an extent the "victims of their own reticence" through the "self—imposed secrecy" of so many of the combatants. Although World War I is exceptionally well documented in historical records and there is a recognized literary heritage that takes the war as its central motif, none draws upon the tunnellers as a primary source. It is almost impossible to write about that war and to generate new meanings, but this is precisely what Faulks does in *Birdsong*. The tunnellers, miners, and clay-kickers who spent most of their time digging below no man's land and who were instrumental in laying the mines that signaled the beginning of one of the greatest battles of the war, have been relegated to the margins of literary discourse. Faulks sees that this is a memory that has been lost and *Birdsong* is his attempt to retrieve their stories from history and from modern memory. He provides a new perspective on an aspect of the war that is virtually unknown and as such, he offers a new reading of the war.

NARRATIVE FORM / STYLE

In *Birdsong* Faulks uses a range of narrative techniques including interior monologue, direct speech, and dramatic irony. The novel is written in third person narrative and an omniscient narrator gives the reader access to the thoughts and feelings of all the main protagonists. The narrator and author are non-intrusive in that there is no direct comment on events or characters and the story is narrated impartially, but the horror of the men's situation and the incompetence of command are made obvious through the narrative. Faulks lets events "speak for themselves" and the strength of his descriptive prose and narrative plot makes perceptible the events surrounding the war without "recourse to the cold tallies of the historian." Despite the omniscient narrator, Faulks chooses to rely on just a handful of characters to recount the events of the novel and as such, actions are seen from a partially restricted point of view. Stephen Wraysford is the central character with the focus of the novel entirely on him, and although Isabelle Azaire, Michael Weir, and Jack Firebrace also have prominent roles, they are frequently only seen in relation to Stephen and where they "take over" the narrative, it is often only fleetingly. The main events are therefore "seen" mainly through Stephen's eyes and this is what makes him such a compelling character.

The novel is presented in six sections: pre-war France in 1910; France in 1916; England in 1978; France in 1917; England in 1978–1979; and France in 1918. The three main time frames intersect and inform each other, with many of the themes of the novel addressed in each time frame. The objective correlative of the different sections is achieved through temporal and geographical shifts in time and place. The use of a non-linear format and the disruption of chronological time allow Faulks to investigate over time the effects of intense feelings and emotions on the main characters. The juxtaposition of the pre-war and the modern sections of the novel are a particularly effective narrative strategy that throws into relief the horrors of the war sections. It is generally acknowledged that the sections set in the contemporary period are not as potent as the other two sections. According to Faulks, this is a deliberate narrative strategy as he intended these sections to be without the immediacy and strength of the others. This is so Elizabeth, Stephen Wraysford's granddaughter, can reflect upon the lack of intensity in her own life and on contemporary life in general.

Faulks's narrative style is both naturalistic and realistic and very much in the manner of the nineteenth century writers he cites as his literary influences. Naturalism is a style of writing that refuses to idealize human experience and shows human endeavor as subject to natural and hostile forces, often beyond the control of the main protagonists. The metaphysical and intellectual aspirations of individuals are seen as meaningless in the face of knowable and unknowable obstacles and, more often than not, the subject matter is one of abjection and despair. This has great resonance for Faulks's writing where he also foregrounds many of these issues. Other naturalist writers such as Emile Zola foreground the experience of the lower classes in their fictions. In *Germinal, La Terre* and *La Débâcle* (which also looks at the horror of war), Zola charts the lives of people conditioned by their environment and by the forces of nature over which they have no control and they are shown as almost animalistic in the process. Zola saw his version of naturalism as somewhat experimental in its alliance of sociological and natural representation, a point that is taken to task by David Lodge in *The Art of Fiction*. Lodge argues that Zola's use of the term "the experimental novel" is misleading and states that "a work of fiction is not a reliable method of verifying or falsifying a hypothesis about society." For Lodge, naturalism is just another style of writing that seeks to unsettle and "defamiliarize" the reader.

Faulks's marriage of abjection and subject matter certainly draws on the naturalist tradition and it is clear that "defamiliarization" is also at work in his writing. However, while he draws upon the naturalist tradition in his novels he has more in common with the realist writers of the nineteenth century. George Gissing's *The Nether World* and Charles Dickens's *Hard Times* for example, are classic realist novels in many ways, but they also draw upon naturalistic devices, such as horror, disgust, and the degradation of human beings by their environment. Both novelists have the working classes as a major force in the narrative and see them to be deserving of representation in literature. Faulks follows a literary tradition here not only in his uses of naturalism and realism, but also in his representation of working-class characters. Jack Firebrace and the "other ranks" are deemed worthy of representation and they are also influenced by their environment and by forces over which they have no control.

Classic realist writers confront "new truths" about the society they write about, drawing upon documentation, sociological detail, and fact, to represent a version of authenticity. This is Faulks's *modus operandi* in *Birdsong* where he unswervingly draws upon "real" moments in history to present his own version of truth through his fiction. He is, ostensibly, portraying things as they "really are" and life as it is "really lived." This is, of course, hugely problematic as these terms raise innumerable questions for our reading of a realist text. *Birdsong* is not "real," it is not even a real representation of the war, it is a literary work that reflects upon the reality of human experience during the war. The realist novel cannot be "an unmanipulated chain of events" as the author has control of the narrative at all times and according to Alison Lee, this often undermines "realist dictates." However, while Faulks's realism may or may not be compromised in his writing it is undoubtedly the case that the descriptions of place, memory, and character in *Birdsong* have resonance of naturalist and realist narrative strategies. Here, for example, is Faulks's evocation of place and memory:

[Stephen] would lie alone, looking up at the ceiling and across to the big fireplace, over to the kitchen range and its black, hanging implements. His thoughts and dreams did not fill up with the big skies of Lincolnshire or the memories of refectory tables and inspections for head lice; nor did he give a backward thought to having abruptly left his employment to import licences, dockets, or bales of cotton unloaded at the East India Docks. He thought about the moment and the next day and the capsule of existence in which he and Isabelle lived, contained within a town and a world of kinds outside. It was an existence he felt had been won by him but in some wider judgement would not be allowed. (p. 88)

This would not be out of place in the classic realism of the nineteenth century. Faulks's narrative thread of a passion that is kindled and then thwarted has an almost direct association to the tragic love stories of the nineteenth century, such as Gustave Flaubert's *Madame Bovary* and Tolstoy's *Anna Karenina*. Simon Schama has in fact labeled him "Flaubert in the Trenches." The comparison is interesting, as Flaubert was also known for his authenticity to detail and his seemingly impersonal narrative style that engages with the morality and the psychological development of his characters. A number of critical responses to Faulks's writing have commented on the very same things. There is also a tradition of war writing that uses the aesthetic of social and historical reality in its portrayal of the "pity of war." Ernest Hemingway's *A Farewell to Arms* and Ford Madox Ford's *The Good Soldier* have similar themes to *Birdsong* in that they use the redemptive nature of rebirth, while Richard Aldington's *Death of a Hero* and Erich Maria Remarque's *All Quiet on the Western Front* both portray the stories of young men, adrift in the horrors of trench warfare. These elements are all very evident in Faulks's writing.

In *Birdsong*, Faulks precedes his debate of war with a story of passionate and tempestuous love that is eventually destroyed by the pressure of guilt promulgated by a society that is suffocating under the repression, hypocrisy, and restrictive codes of morality of the *petit bourgeoisie*. The sociological narrative thread in *Birdsong* exposes the indiscriminate exploitation of the textile workers in a time of crisis and recession in the industrial confines of pre-war Amiens. Lucien Lebrun, "one of the hot-headed leaders of the strike," gives a passionate speech to the workers in the textile factory that gives voice to "the hardships endured by the strikers' families and the working conditions that had driven them to their extreme action" (p. 41). Faulks shows the poverty and exploitation that was rife throughout the plain of Picardy in a storyline that foreshadows the appalling treatment and subjugation of the "ordinary" man in the trenches of World War I. The opening scenes in the first section of the novel afford lyrical yet unsettling descriptions of time and place, where Faulks presents the stifling and foreboding atmosphere of the backwaters of the Somme, in pre-war France:

Stephen felt hot and thickheaded from the wine. He was repelled by the water gardens; their hectic abundance seemed to him close to the vegetable fertility of death. The brown water were murky and shot through with the scurrying of rats from the banks where the earth had been dug out of trenches and held back by elaborate boarding.... What was held to be a place of beauty was a stagnation of living tissue which could not be saved from decay. (p. 37)

The foreshadowing of the events of the war and the horrors to come are evoked by the descriptive and symbolic nature of Faulks's writing. His writing in this section is steeped in dramatic irony and it is often deeply moving in its portrayal of the helplessness of the human condition in the face of overwhelming forces. His writing is also sensual and erotically charged at other moments. The simple act of Stephen's leg brushing against Isabelle's in the confines of the boat on the canal is given a frisson, a pleasurable sensation that charges the senses. This sensation of desire is likened to "an impulse towards death"(p. 38) and is indicative of the way the affair will end. One of the main themes of the novel is the transgressing of boundaries and Stephen and Isabelle's transgression of sexual and societal boundaries takes them beyond the limits of acceptability on a journey that symbolizes the loss of innocence of a whole generation.

Faulks's narrative style throughout is palimpsestic and layered, with the different strands juxtaposed in the internal accounts of personal experiences. He uses the typical postmodern literary device of split narrative and multiple viewpoints through the use of letters and internal monologue. The letters are apparently free standing, separate from yet an intrinsic part of the story. This narrative device is used in other historiographic novels such as D.M. Thomas's *The White Hotel* where he uses postcards in the same way, or by Doris Lessing in *Briefing for a Descent into Hell* where letters are used to reconstruct the character of a man who loses his memory. The letters in *Birdsong* allow the narrative to be reconstructed outside the world of the novel, to allow different "voices" to be heard and to gain insight into the psyche of the characters. They contrast sharply with the conditions the men at the Front had to deal with and are indicative of the withholding of information about the real horrors of the war:

Michael Weir wrote:
    Dear Mother and Father, We are going to attack. . . . Morale is very high. We will expect that this push will end the war. It is unlikely that

many of the enemy will have survived our bombardment. . . . Don't worry about me please . . . there is nothing further I need . . . (p. 177)

Tipper wrote:

Dear Mum and Dad, They sent me back to join my pals and I am so proud to be back with and them. It's a terrific show with all the bands and the men from other units. Our guns are putting on a display like Firework Night. We are going to attack and we can't wait to let Fritz have it! The General says we don't expect no resistance at all because our guns have finished them off. . . . Don't worry about me. I am not frightened of what is waiting for me. . . . I won't let you down. . . . From your son John (p. 178).

Byrne wrote:

Dear Ted, These are a special few lines in case we don't meet again. We are going to attack tomorrow, everything is absolutely thumbs-up merry and bright and trusting to the best of luck. . . . Here's hoping it is au revoir and not goodbye. . . . Your loving brother Albert. Cheer-oh Ted, don't worry about me I'm OK. (p. 179)

Faulks's writing is emotionally charged at this point and the "ordinary" men are shown to have faith that they can transcend the horrors that we know await them. The dramatic irony inherent in the letters renders the scene almost heartbreaking in its expression of the men's naivete and hope.

Faulks also uses symbolism in his writing, not always as successfully as his other narrative strategies. A symbol commonly represents a metaphysical entity or state of being and it usually "stands" for something else. The use of symbols in literature is widespread and prevailing but it frequently engenders an ambiguity of meaning. It is not always clear what these elements "stand for" in the Faulks's novel either. Bird imagery predominates in this aspect of his writing: nightingales, blackbirds, pigeons, and canaries all feature prominently, as does Stephen's nightmares and fear of birds. It cannot be that they simply represent freedom and entrapment. The color red

is a motif that is used again and again throughout the novel, either
in descriptions of Isabelle's clothing and jewelery, in the room
Isabelle and Stephen make love in, and of course in the color of
blood (women's menstrual blood and the blood of the soldiers). His
use of three German characters at the end of the war is also highly
symbolic in that one, Levi, is Jewish. This must be seen as an
indication of what happens over the next twenty years to the Jews of
Europe, but its application is fairly heavy handed. In *Birdsong* the
symbolism is rather awkward and self-conscious, for example, the
birth of a child is a rather cliched symbol of rebirth and hope and
the birds are obviously a synecdoche (the substitution of a part of
nature to represent nature as a whole). The juxtaposition of nature
and mechanization (war) is realized in many ways throughout the
novel and the themes of redemption and rebirth are better realized
in the first two time frames of the novel. The novel could do
without much of this symbolism as the strength of Faulks's writing
lies in his lyrical prose and in the meticulous nature of his descriptions.

CHARACTER

The great tradition of realist writing is that it is driven by character
and plot. David Lodge maintains that "character is arguably the
most important single component of the novel" and in many cases
this is irrefutable. The success of a novel frequently stands or falls
by the strengths and weaknesses its characterization. Characters are
not "real" people but are imaginary, invented persons who are given
human qualities and who, in a realist novel, behave in a manner
that mostly conforms to human conduct. Character is most specifically realized through description, action, and dialogue, commonly
known as "showing and telling." "Showing" is achieved by the

direct speech acts of the characters and "telling" in the manner of narration. The facets of a character are additionally perceived through characterization and the manner in which the author creates sympathy or antagonism towards the protagonists. One reason for *Birdsong*'s overwhelming popularity is the strength of Faulks's portrayal of character in his main protagonists. The morality and motivation of the main characters are explored without didactic comment or authorial speculation and this undoubtedly empowers the reader in that they can make up their own minds about characters and the reasons why they act as they do. Faulks contends that *Birdsong* has six main characters, three males and three females, and this presupposes that he gives equal weight to his male and female protagonists. But it is obvious that Stephen Wraysford, Jack Firebrace, and Michael Weir are the dominant characters, while out of the female characters it is only Isabelle who predominates and Jeanne and Elizabeth are relegated to the position of eyewitnesses to history. There are *dominant* characters in the different time frames of the novel such as Isabelle Azaire, Jack Firebrace, and Michael Weir in the war sections and Elizabeth in the contemporary section, but it is clear at all times where the main focus of the novel lies.

In any novel that incorporates a broad sweep of twentieth century history there are bound to be numerous characters, major and minor, some not as effectively drawn as others and some that border on caricature. This is simply because there is not enough space to engage in exhaustive descriptions of multifarious characters. In *Birdsong* there are many "minor" characters that appear in all three time frames. These are predominantly male and exist in communities of men where the friendships/relationships are important as social signifiers of patriarchal authority and the need for homosocial relations between men. This is not surprising as the predominant theme and motif of the novel is war and the effects it has on the men who fought in it. In *Male Myths and Icons*, Roger Horrocks argues there is a desire between men for maleness and masculinity that is realized through the various relationships that exist between men. These relationships are powerfully realized in the novel and they can be seen in a number of situations. For example, Stephen talks of boys who "prefer to be together so that they can at least share the new things they are discovering about the world" (p. 53) and Jack Firebrace looks on other soldiers "with love and gratitude" as "they understood the difficulties of a man who had been stretched too far" (p. 110). This reliance on other men predominates in the emotionally charged relationships between the men during war and it is an important motif in the representation of male characters in the novel.

Minor characters such as Azaire, Bérard, and Lebrun that appear in the pre-war section; Hunt, Brennan, Byrne, Levi, Gray, and Shaw who are in the war section, and Robert and Stuart in the contemporary setting, all contribute to the narrative. It is possible to see, through an examination of these protagonists, how facets of character emerge through the narrative itself, driven by speech and actions in certain situations. The omniscient nature of the narration provides insight into their lives and their behavior. The most obvious sense of a character is often drawn from physical description, such as the descriptions of Bérard as "a heavily set grey-haired man in his fifties" (p. 6) or Lucien Lebrun with his "candid blue eyes and wavy, brown hair" (p. 41). Berard is shown to be a pompous bully who "was clearly used to having his own way" (p. 8) and who "took it as his burden to act as a conductor. To bring in the different voices, and then summarize what they had contributed" in any gathering. (p. 7). From these descriptions and narratorial comments it is possible to see that he is a character who is full of his own importance. Azaire is shown as being harsh in business, but a coward: "What these strikers need . . . is for someone to call their bluff. I'm not prepared to see my business stagnate because of the gross demands of a few idle men. Some owner has to have the strength to stand up to them and sack the whole lot" (p. 11). This is confirmed by his behavior towards his wife: "He did not love her but he wanted her to be more responsive towards him . . . if she could not love him then at least she should be frightened of him" (p. 65). In this way, character provides insight into the narrative and the representations offer a glimpse of the underlying traits of a character that will have some bearing on the events of the novel.

Stephen Wraysford is the major force in all three parts of the novel and he is a "typical" character in a realist novel. In *The Meaning of Contemporary Realism*, Georg Lukács states that a character is typical "when his innermost being is determined by objective forces in society" and Stephen is ("typical") in that forces outside of his control determine his fate. His story also dominates the narrative, even in the contemporary story where he is absent, as it is his history that is excavated from the past by his granddaughter. In his representation of Stephen, Faulks uses traditional narrative techniques of introducing his character through physical description and personal characteristics. He is shown as:

a tall figure with hands thrust into his pockets, his eyes patient and intent, the angle of his body that of a youthful indifference cultivated by willpower and necessity. It was a face which in turn most people treated cautiously, unsure whether its ambivalent expressions would resolve themselves into passion or acquiescence. (p. 12)

The vicissitudes of his early life are shown in the narrator's knowing comments regarding his willpower that is a "product of necessity." Through this form of characterization it is immediately shown that there has been trauma somewhere in his life and his actions will be determined by this. His character is drawn through reflection on the past, from information he gives to Isabelle, and from other character's reaction to him. He is initially drawn as a young man who is cautious and in control. The narrator informs us he has a "sense of secrecy" about him and that he had "slowly learned to breathe and keep calm, not to trust his responses, but to wait and be watchful." However, Stephen is caught up in a passion that is outside his control and his actions towards Isabelle Azaire do not reflect this description of him. This leads us to question the reliability of the narrator. Stephen is also "mastered by . . . feeling" and although he is drawn irresistibly into his highly wrought affair, he is also able to detach himself from it, psychologically. He exhibits an inquiring mind and "an overwhelming sense of curiosity" (p. 70) and he will not rest until he knows where events will end. This is what enables him to survive, this and the fact that he has a vested interest in preserving something of himself. He survives both the trauma of the desertion of Isabelle and the horrors of the war because "he hardened his heart" and through an act of "almost physical willpower, as he compelled the compassion to go out of him" (p. 78). Stephen is thus shown to be a typical character, one that is a complex and one that is often contradictory and frequently paradoxical and ambivalent. He is not necessarily a charismatic character or even that likeable, but he is compelling. He has great empathy for all the soldiers, even the Germans, and tells Jack Firebrace at one stage, "every one of the men we've killed is someone's son. Do you think of that when you see them dead? Do you wonder what their mothers thought when they first held them to their breast—that they would end like this?" (p. 111). Stephen is our eyewitness to history and as such he remains central to the plot and to the themes of the novel. His compassion, his desire to control his life, to conquer his fear and to stifle any hint of emotion, reflects a version of quintessential "Britishness" and manliness that Faulks seems to hold dear.

Faulks clearly uses the characters in his novel as narrative devices to facilitate the moral thesis of his writing. If Stephen is the central character upon whom the action is predicated then other characters such as Isabelle Azaire, Michael Weir, and Jack Firebrace are significant, but peripheral. Isabelle is important in that she is a conduit for Stephen's sensory experiences. The passion they share is the faculty through which Stephen experiences the internal and external worlds of physical sensation. He alone recognizes an unconscious desire in Isabelle and feels certain "there was some keener physical life than she was actually living in the calm, restrictive rooms of her husband's house" (p. 19). Isabelle is "animated by a different kind of rhythm from that which beat in her husband's blood" (p. 18). This is a very telling description in that it offers a view of her as a sexual being. The narrator reflects upon Isabelle's actions and thoughts, "she was choking with passion for him . . . currents of desire and excitement that she had not known or thought about for years flooded in her" and she is shown to act on those feelings as "she wanted him to bring alive what she had buried and to demean, destroy her fabricated self"(p. 48). Faulks, like Thomas Hardy, uses the female body as a metaphor for lost innocence. Isabelle is a Hardyesque character who embodies the passion and the spirit of many of Hardy's heroines. In many ways, Isabelle embodies the sensuality and repressed sexuality of Sue Bridehead in *Jude the Obscure*. Stephen describes "the pulse" of Isabelle, who palpitates with intense sexual longing in the same way that Sue Bridehead "tremble[s] through her limbs" with passion. But like Tess in *Tess of the D'Urbervilles*, the fate of a country is written on her body and her demise is preordained. She will be condemned by her actions and her passion will eventually destroy her. Her flight to Germany to be with her lover ensures that she will succumb to the fate of so many people after the war, the influenza pandemic.

Isabelle is also defined by other character's responses to her and this differs in perception through the application of various narrative "lenses." Azaire, for example describes Isabelle as "a woman of nervous temperament" who suffers from "headaches and various minor maladies" (p. 11). Her husband labels Isabelle a "hysteric," a fate that befell many women of her generation. There are elements of dramatic irony in these descriptions; not only do we know more about Isabelle than Azaire through the omniscient narrator, we also have the distance of time to understand how the repression of instinctual feelings manifests itself in women. Isabelle is an important character in that the passion between her and Stephen shows to what uses the human body can be put. She also transgresses the boundaries of what is considered "decent" behavior and shows that passion can transcend morality. Isabelle feels "shame and impropriety" at her behavior but is more excited by that feeling than anything else. At the height of her passionate affair with Stephen she feels "no guilt . . . she could do whatever she wanted" (p. 49). Isabelle calls him "a boy, the dearest boy," and despite her initial misgivings about her actions, she knows that by giving herself to him in the way she has "she would have him always" (p. 51). Isabelle makes Stephen feel "awkward, half-undressed; it was as though she had treated him like a boy and taunted him" (p. 60). Again, the reliability of the narrator is questioned as Isabelle's thoughts and actions tend to define her as more knowing and sexually aware than Stephen suspects. Society puts value on female qualities such as modesty and decency, but Isabelle transcends these confining constructs, if only for a short period. Through her, Faulks explores the physical and emotional side of women's material life, but he also shows how strong ideological dictates are:

Isabelle began to look with regret towards her parents and their continuing lives. The coming child had already begun to still her most restless expectation. The need satisfied in her was so deep that she had not previously been aware of it. It was as though she had become conscious of a starving hunger only after having eaten. It seemed to alter the levels and balances of her needs . . . it brought doubts about what she had done, it made her want to be reunited with her family. (p. 90)

Isabelle is also a fairly complex character. She is shown to flout all known conventions in her affair and subsequent flight with Stephen but she feels uneasy about the things she and Stephen do. It is only after they have left Amiens and are living together that she begins to doubt her actions. Faulks seems to imply that all she needs as a woman to make her feel whole is a child. Passion is not enough, obviously, as she also acknowledges that "without the stimulus of fear and prohibition, her desire had slackened" (p. 90). Isabelle is a finely drawn character in many respects but she seems to be idealized on one hand and made to appear slightly shallow on the other. It is typical in many novels for a female character to die when she transgresses moral and social boundaries. Isabelle *has* to suffer and her suffering is written on her body in the scarring on her face and the immobility of her limbs.

A novel, or a text, engenders readings that either confirm or confront dominant ideological beliefs and when male writers define women sexually it is usually in terms of opinion and judgement and Faulks, really, is no exception to the rule. There are many questions to be raised about Faulks's portrayal of Isabelle in particular and about his representation of women in general (see discussion questions). Elizabeth and Isabelle both appear to be self-determined but they are, in reality, women who are defined by their biological function. Elizabeth in particular is a very contradictory character. She understands, for example, that for women a career and marriage are not mutually exclusive, and she is the mistress of a married man who pretends she does not exist. She also tells a friend that she is not bothered if he never leaves his wife. A strong, independent

woman you might think. But, Elizabeth demands that Robert tell
her when he intends to marry her, which immediately undermines
the reliability of her statements. Elizabeth acknowledges that she
may have chosen someone unobtainable because "he did not
threaten her independence" (p. 222) but this does not explain all
the contradictions in the novel. She also proclaims she "has to stop
walking" when she sees a small child, as "her guts turn over . . . and
[she] has to take several deep breaths because [her] body is yearning
so strongly" for a baby (p. 214). Elizabeth and Isabelle never forego
this drive towards motherhood and this reflects more on Faulks's
view of women perhaps than anything else. However, Elizabeth is
an important part of the novel as it is her need to find out about
her family's history that drives the narrative in the contemporary
time frame. She feels there is a danger of losing touch with history,
and her search for a connection with what has gone before and her
insistence of the presence of the past as being significant mirrors
Faulks's own sentiments. As such, she embodies much of his way of
thinking.

Michael Weir and Jack Firebrace are more convincing as characters than Isabelle or Elizabeth. The framing device of two illicit
affairs and two pregnancies is problematic in many ways but they
do render more starkly the horrors of the war story. Perhaps there is
something in Faulks's predominantly male upbringing that helps in
his moving portrayal of men and their relationships. The war section
introduces both Michael and Jack who are beneath "several hundred thousand tons of France," one digging the tunnels and one
supervising the proceedings (p. 99). The claustrophobic, dangerous
conditions in which the tunnellers work are shown in harsh relief
by the immediate explosion beneath the ground and the images of
shattered male bodies. Jack, who was responsible for listening out
for movement in the tunnel, is philosophical about the incident:

"He did not berate himself for failing to identify the sound of a German tunnel. He had done his best, and the men might have died anyway, perhaps in a worse way, with gas in their lungs or lying beyond help in no-man's-land" (p. 103). This pragmatic approach to life and death is a symptom of how immune the men become to the horrors they witness. Jack Firebrace's response to the horrors around him is significant. He feels he is immune but reacts strongly at the thought of his own death:

[He] began to tremble. . . . He would fall like the millions of the dead who had gone down into the mud; baker's boys from Saxony, farm labourers from France and factory workers from Lancashire, so much muscle and blood in the earth.

He could not look on this possibility without shaking. . . . The indifference he had cultivated, however, was to the extermination of the enemy, his colleagues and his friends; he was not, he now admitted to himself, indifferent to the prospect of his own death. (p. 107)

In episodes such as this Faulks brings to the surface the fear of the men and evokes the dreadful pity of the war. It helps that Jack Firebrace is such a sympathetic and memorable character. He is unusual, a wholly believable and fully rounded working-class character. He has a native intelligence and intuition and he is predisposed to endure the suffering with which he is burdened. He says "I have made this mistake in my life . . . not once but twice I have loved someone more than my heart would bear" (p. 276). He understands the dual nature of the love he feels for his son and for his friend. He also has great dignity which he retains until the end, unlike Michael Weir, who appears to be completely reliant on Stephen for his peace of mind and who eventually breaks down under the strain of the horror he sees all around him. Jack has the intelligence to understand his situation and until the closing mo-

ments of the war, he has the will to survive. Jack Firebrace epito-
mizes the notion of a soldier hero, and it is made clear by Faulks in
his characterization of Jack and the "other ranks" that the soldiers
who carried the burden of the war are the real heroes.

FAITH/HUMAN ENDURANCE/SUPERSTITION

In the pitiless activity that is war there is an extraordinary need for
belief in the altruism of the human condition. Faith and its concomitant themes of human endurance and loss of faith as a result
of loss of innocence are two of *Birdsong*'s most enduring themes. In
The Great War and Modern Memory, Paul Fussell devotes a chapter
to myth, ritual, and romance and shows how important these are
for the soldiers. The war, he says, was a place of "secrets, conver-
sions, metamorphoses and rebirths." It is ironic in many ways that
the first mechanized war, a war that represents the move towards
capitalism, industrialization, and a mechanized society should result
in what Fussell calls, a "plethora of very un-modern superstitions,
talismans, wonders, miracles, relics, legends and rumors." Many
soldiers believe they can become invincible as long as they keep
faith, and in order to sustain this belief they develop superstitious
rituals. Fussell suggests that soldiers and war protagonists go through
a number of stages in certainty, each of which involves "miracles
and dangers" in a crucial test of faith. These rituals may involve
"magical numbers, secret murmurings and whispers and perilous
encounters." Faulks shows how superstition plays an important part
in the soldiers' lives and in their tests of faith. The men of the
"other ranks" are usually the most superstitious; the miners play a
game underground called "Fritz" upon which outcome they believe
their fate rests and they also bet on how quickly cans in the trenches

fill up with water. The outcome of both of these rituals is then seen as an omen for survival.

Both Fussell and Faulks tell stories of men who go into no man's land at night and quite brazenly smoke cigarettes when they know it will make them a "sitting target" for German snipers. This is an act of bravado in the face of danger but it can also be seen as a test of faith. The nightly ritual carries within it its own protection as far as the men are concerned. There are also other rituals: when Jack Firebrace goes into the officer's dugout he sees on the table "five playing cards laid out in the shape of a star, face down, with thin trails of sand between them. In the centre of the formation was a carved wooden figure and a stump of candle" (p. 109). Michael Weir is shown to be as superstitious as the "other ranks" in that he relies on Stephen's use of "voodoo" to predict his survival chances. Ellis, a new officer, is unconvinced at the role it plays in Michael's well-being but Stephen explains: "This is voodoo I invented to pass the long hours. Weir likes it. It makes him think someone cares about him. It's better to have a malign providence than an indifferent one" (p. 232). In other words, Faulks shows that it is better for the men, whoever they are, to believe in something rather than in nothing at all. Faulks shows how games and rituals help the men to survive in a situation where conventional religion has not much to offer. He also shows how the army tries to keep religious faith among the soldiers. Horrocks the padre fulfills his theological duties, he takes communion but he only operates behind the front line. Again, Faulks shows how it is left to men such as Stephen Wraysford and Jack Firebrace to do their "duty as a Christian" and say prayers for the dead. In *Birdsong* the characters show great faith in that they have a strong belief in the power or powers that control human destiny. The soldiers are superstitious but need their faith to sustain them. On the eve of battle they flock around the padre, "non-believers finding faith in fear" (p. 175).

The soldiers are also trained to have faith in their commanding officers. The irony that is implicit in this belief is strongly realized in Faulks's narrative. Gray understands the need for men to believe in their officers and to have faith that all will be well. He instructs Stephen to tell his men that:

The artillery lays down a protective barrage in front of you. You advance at walking pace behind the barrage. When it lifts you take your objectives, then wait for it to begin again. It provides protection for you all the way. The German wire is already cut and many of their guns destroyed. Casualties will be ten per cent. (p. 176)

Gray, however, knows there has been a "cockup" and advises his officers not to tell the men what they will really be facing, just to "pray for the men." The men talk about the superstitious dread of the significance of certain events but Gray tells Stephen that the lives of the soldiers depend on strategy and tactics, not on superstitious rituals. This is deeply ironic as time and time again the soldiers are let down by their officer's tactics. Gray is inconsistent in his beliefs. He argues that there is a human need to believe in something that exists outside themselves and states that "if the world is broken up by too much reality the need becomes internalised." He sees Stephen's use of superstition and voodoo as a result of "too much reality" as a child, but he does not acknowledge the adult need to believe in something that has an existence outside normal comprehension.

According to Lyn Macdonald, after months and years of abomination the men of the Western Front began to develop a new attitude of fatalism. They believed that if a bullet had their name on it they would "get it" and if it had not, they would be all right. This attitude almost made life bearable for the soldiers, and it is this fatalism that makes many of the battle scenes almost unbearable as they are read with the knowledge that most of the men will not survive. Among the compelling and distressing scenes the book evokes, it is the depiction of the battle that was the Somme in 1916 that is the most terrible. The men are smashed by shells, raked with machine-gun fire, and trapped behind the German wire that has not been cut. Stephen sees then as a "long, wavering line of khaki, primitive dolls progressing in tense deliberate steps, going down with a silent flap of arms, replaced, falling, continuing as walking into a gale (p. 181). Jack Firebrace and Arthur Shaw watch the battle from a distance and see "men from every corner walking, powerless, into an engulfing storm . . . young men dying in quantities they had not dreamed possible." Faulks succinctly evokes the excessive horror of this appalling event. Here he also touches on theological trauma as the padre pulls off his cross and throws it away from him: "Please God let it stop" is the sentiment, but both Horrocks and Jack Firebrace know it will not. This scene is important as it not only signifies a loss of faith, but a loss of innocence in the face of total abjection and horror. Jack sees innocence as "a powerful quality of goodness that was available to all people: it was perhaps what the prayer book called a means of grace, or a hope of glory" (p. 159). The men who survive are empty vessels whose "lives with their memories and loves . . . [are] spinning and vomiting into the ground"(p. 186). For these men nothing will ever be the same again for they see there is no glory or grace in what they undergo.

In the opening section of the novel faith has a slightly different connotation. It takes the form of both religious belief and of loyalty and obedience. Stephen and Isabelle transgress the boundaries of faith that sustain the values and beliefs of the society they live in, and they both realize that this will not be allowed in the wider context of their lives. Isabelle's faith makes her seek forgiveness for her adultery and she feels she must do penance. She feels she has to be punished for her behavior and as she contemplates her fate in a local church she philosophizes about the nature of faith and sacrifice:

She looked to the altar where a wooden crucifix was lit by candles. . . . She thought how prosaically physical this suffering had been; the punctured skin on forehead, feet, hands, the parting of flesh with nails and steel. When even the divine sacrifice had been expressed in such terms, it was sometimes hard to imagine in what manner precisely human life was supposed to exceed the limitations of pulse, skin and decomposition. (p. 93)

Isabelle's meditation on the limits of human life is determined by the pleasures of the body, but this moment concisely foreshadows the destruction of the human body in the war section. Stephen's moment of epiphany in the cathedral may also be seen as a result of faith, it came after all, from his "contemplation of the church," but it is interesting in that "it had its own clarity." It may be a prophetic vision of the future as he imagines "the terrible piling up of the dead . . . row on row, the deep rotting earth hollowed out to hold them, while the efforts of the living . . . were no more than the beat of a wing against the weight of time" (p. 59). The weight of time is important for Faulks and it is clear that he wishes to connect to the past, to "keep the chain of experience intact" (p. 326). As such, the novel is a threnody, a hymn of lamentation, a test of faith and an act of reconciliation and remembrance for the men who fought and died so tragically in the horror that was the Western Front.

Faith is shown in many different ways throughout the novel, through theological belief, allegiance, commitment, dedication and loyalty and through the redemptive power of love. It is Elizabeth who is the moral center of the contemporary story, and Faulks uses her character to articulate many of his own thoughts about the past. She is important in that she reconstructs the past and rescues "some vital connection" to what has gone before, in much the same way that Faulks has with his novel. She rediscovers the idea of faith and human redemption through her unraveling of the past in her grandfather's war notebooks and in the birth of her child, John, named in an act of faith after the dead son of Jack Firebrace. Love is one of the prevailing themes, not only in the love stories between Isabelle and Stephen and Elizabeth and Robert, but in the belief that love (in its many forms) can heal. Jeanne, through her love, reawakens Stephen's faith when he loses touch with the reality of his life. She tells him that he can find what has been lost and that "nothing is beyond redemption" (p. 349). Faulks implies throughout the novel that it is love that is the redemptive power for humanity. Françoise tells Elizabeth that "where there is real love between people . . . the details don't matter" (p. 399), and Stephen reflects that his love for Isabelle made him "able to hear other things in the world" (p. 382). Jack also finds meaning in the love he feels for his son:

I loved that boy. Every hair of him, every pore of his skin. I would have killed a man who so much as laid a hand on him. My world was in his face . . . I treasured each word he gave me. I made myself remember each thing he did, the way he turned his head, his way of saying things. . . . He was from another world, he was a blessing too great for me. (p. 365)

The strength of feeling he has for his son allows Jack to unlock the dreadful passion and pity he feels for the "sons" who die. Finally, it is the knowledge of the loss of so many sons that makes Jack finally lose his will to live.

Birdsong in many ways is a novel of ordeal and a novel of quest and self-discovery. The novel of ordeal, according to Mikhail Bakhtin, "is constructed as a series of tests of the main heroes, tests of their fidelity, valor, bravery, virtue, nobility, sanctity and so on . . .

the struggle and testing of the hero." He also states that, "[this] always begins where a deviation from the normal social and biographical course of life begins, and it ends where life resumes its normal course." Many men in the novel believe they are fighting a brave and noble cause when they arrive in France and it is only when they see how life in the trenches deviates from "normality," even the normality of warfare that they begin to develop their own tests of faith. The novel explores the levels of endurance and the levels of human endeavor in the most abhorrent and disgusting situations. The men are forced to look at suffering and death in its crudest form. A long section of the novel accentuates the horrors of no man's land and the search for bodies and survivors:

They moved low towards a mine crater where bodies had lain for weeks uncollected. "Try to lift him." No sound of machine guns or snipers, though their ears were braced for noise. "Take his arms." The incomprehensible order through the gas mouthpiece. The arms came away softly.

The horror is intensified in the image that is evoked by the disintegration of the male body. The narrative continues:

On Weir's collar a large rat trailing something red down his back. A crow disturbed, lifting its black body up suddenly, battering the air with its big wings. Coker, Barlow shaking their heads under the assault of risen flies coming up, transforming black skin of corpses into green by their absence. The roaring of Goddard's vomit made them laugh. . . . Bright and sleek on liver, a rat emerged from the abdomen and flopped fatly over the ribs, glutted with pleasure. . . . Brennan anxiously stripping a torso with no head. He clasped it with both hands, dragged legless up from the crater, his fingers vanishing into buttered green flesh. It was his brother. (p. 281)

Faulks's writing style here is fragmented and spare and it is extremely effectual in its portrayal of the gruesome and macabre situation the men find themselves in. The men encounter such horror and devastation that they become immune to it. Stephen Wraysford certainly takes strength from the horrors he endures:

> He grew used to the sight and smell of torn human flesh. He watched the men harden to the mechanical slaughter. There seemed to him a great breach of nature which no one had the power to stop.
>
> He could protest or he could go with it. He tuned himself to killing. He tried to be fearless in the hope that it would comfort the other men, whose dazed and uncomprehending faces he saw through the blood and the noise. If this was to be permitted, reported, glossed over, then at what level of activity, he wondered, could they stop? He came to believe that much worse was to come; that there would be annihilation on a scale the men themselves had not dreamed of. (p. 132)

Stephen's faith lies in his will to survive. This is seen on countless occasions but is most prominent in his near-death experience which occurred after he was blown up in one of the tunnels:

> He heard a voice, not human, but clear and urgent. It was the sound of his life leaving him. Its tone was mocking. It offered him, instead of the peace he longed for, the possibility of return. At this late stage he could go back to his body and to the brutal perversion of life that was lived in the turned soil and torn flesh of the war; he could, if he made the effort of courage and will, come back to the awkward, compromised and unconquerable existence that made up human life on earth. The voice was calling him; it appealed to his sense of shame and of curiosity unfulfilled: but if he did not heed it he would surely die. (p. 144)

Stephen is "reborn" at this moment but his act of faith is sustained out of curiosity rather than any deeply held religious belief. The novel proliferates with rebirthing and redemptive experiences: when Jack and Stephen are trapped underground, for example, Jack feels

he will be saved and that "Stephen would deliver him"(p. 359).
Stephen, Michael, and Jack have many treacherous journeys
through the narrow, blood stained walls of the tunnels and emerge
again and again, reborn into the horrors of the world. It is argued
that human suffering frequently brings human nobility to the surface and in the novel Faulks shows how this nobility is realized in
future generations. The birth of Elizabeth's son at the end of the
book is the final act of reconciliation with the past and a redemptive
act of atonement for the horrific experiences of so many sons.

THE SOLDIER HERO AND THE CRISIS OF MASCULINITY

In *Birdsong* Faulks gives voice to men, who, according to Siegfried
Sassoon, "were victims of conspiracy among . . . politicians . . . military caste . . . people making money out of the war and the compla-
cency of those willing to watch sacrifices of others while they sit
safely at home." Faulks illustrates the constraints and expectations
placed on men during war and reveals the predicament of soldiers
whose "masculinity" is undermined by the horror and degradation
they endure in the trenches. In *Soldier Heroes: British Adventure,
Empire and the Imagining of Masculinity*, Graham Dawson states
that "the soldier is a quintessential figure of masculinity" and that
"the nation plays its part in constituting preferred forms of masculinity." In other words, at times of war the nation expects its soldiers to
be strong, heroic, and to be what is commonly known as "real men."
The men in the trenches of the Western Front, however, are in the
most unsuitable position to perform heroic feats of masculinity. As
Sandra Gilbert states "the war to which so many had gone in the
hope of becoming heroes ended up emasculating them, depriving
them of autonomy, confining them as closely as any Victorian
woman had been confined." Faulks shows how men who are inac-

tive for great amounts of time are rendered passive in a subterranean world of trenches and tunnels. The claustrophobic world he creates shows very precisely how soldiers are "unmanned" during moments of crisis and confinement.

Elaine Showalter states that when men are silenced and immobilized, they are "forced, like women, to express their conflicts through the body" and it is this breakdown of the human body and mind that is deemed "unmanly." In *Birdsong*, Faulks shows how men are broken down by their experiences in the trenches. These breakdowns take many different forms: Hunt breaks down and sobs in the tunnels; Michael Weir breaks down while under shell fire; Tipper cannot control his fear in the trenches; and Stephen very nearly attacks a young prostitute while suffering from shell shock. The fact that many of the soldiers find their breakdown an emasculating experience confirms the notion of a prescribed form of masculinity. "Real" men were not supposed to break down under any circumstances, although, as Peter Middleton states, a "real man" is a fantasy ideal representing aspirations neither recognisable, nor necessarily desirable." The terrors of the war and the expectations of manliness on the part of the soldier combine to produce cases of male hysteria in large numbers of men, a fact that is acknowledged in Faulks's portrayal. In the novel he offers a compelling and forceful evocation of the personal experiences of men during war and a powerful expression of masculinity in crisis.

In writing the story of Stephen Wraysford and the men who fought alongside him, Faulks presents his own memorial to that "lost" generation of men who fought in the war that was supposed "to end all wars." In the novel, however, the idea of the soldier as an archetypal warrior hero is rendered obsolete. In his preface to Richard Aldington's *Death of a Hero*, Christopher Ridgway writes that soldiers are heroes, albeit reluctant heroes. He states:

they are outcasts; their heroism consists in their comradeship and their resistance to the odious world that will insist upon appropriating them, posthumously as patron saints. Those who are dispossessed are repossessed falsely, after their deaths.

Faulks, like Aldington, obviously recognizes a new brand of heroism inherent in the soldiers and although in many ways he does penance through his writing for the hundreds of thousands of men who died, Faulks does not fall into the trap of easy glorification. In order to "repossess" their lives accurately he draws upon memory and history and the recollections of some of the isolated horrors of the war. He gives a clear indication of the appalling conditions the men in the tunnels had to put up with:

There was a roar in the tunnel and a huge ball of rock and earth blew past them. It took four men with it, their heads and limbs blown away and mixed with the rushing soil. . . . Jack saw part of Turner's face and hair still attached to a piece of skull rolling to a halt. . . . There was an arm with a corporal's stripe on it near his feet. . . . Jack took Evan's shoulder. "Come on boy. Come on now." (p. 101)

In the light of these conditions it is understandable that many soldiers suffer from shell shock and neurasthenia. Ann Whitehead states that neurasthenia or shell shock originates "in a traumatic moment of shock without effect" and that in someone who is suffering from shell shock "history represents a past that has not been experienced at the time which it occurred." Faulks shows how this manifests itself in the behavior of Stephen Wraysford. The appalling events he experiences do not seem to affect him unduly, but his shell shock manifests itself in many different ways. Most tellingly, the traumatic events are brought to the fore when he returns to England on leave:

Brightly illuminated scenes from the last two or three years occurred at random in his mind. Incidents and men he had forgotten recurred with vivid immediacy, and then were gone. He tried to pull himself back from the lurid sequence of memories. He kept seeing Douglas falling off the stretcher on to the slippery floor of the trench as a shell landed; he could hear the lifeless thump of his passive body. A man he had forgotten called Studd, came back to his mind, his helmet blown back and his scalp raked by machine gun bullets as he bent to help another man who had fallen. ... It seemed to him extraordinary that he should be feeling the shock now, when he was safe in a tranquil English village. (p. 290).

Whitehead also states that the events that cause shell shock are often dislocated from historical process and the affect with which it is associated "surges back uncontrollably into the present moment, causing a painful and vivid belated experiencing of the trauma." It is clear that Stephen is suffering from shell shock in this moment but it is obviously not recognized. This manifests itself again and again in Stephen's behavior:

When he looked at the girl's upper body, the ribs and the spine he thought of the shell casing that stuck from Reeves's abdomen; he thought of the hole in Douglas's shoulder where he had pressed his hand through almost to the lung.

His tenderness was replaced at first by a shuddering revulsion. Then his mind emptied. There was only this physical mass. He was losing control. ... The daughter's body was no more than animal matter, less dear, less valuable than the flesh of men he had seen die. (pp. 165–166)

Stephen's breakdown is assuaged at the last minute, but he draws his knife on the prostitute and marks her skin with it. Stephen's enforced masculinity and his repression of emotion, and the denial of both sexual feelings and fear both before and during the war manifests in his actions towards the young woman. He does not allow himself to feel emotion or to express his fears and this is why he breaks down.

In Britain, the expectations of a nation rested firmly on the men at the Western Front, and public opinion was not interested in defeat or in men who break down under fire. In *They Called it Passchendaele*, Lyn Macdonald claims that during the war "emotion was riding high," at least in Britain, where the "flags waved and the drums beat and the newspapers trumpeted forth glory in every edition." Society as a whole did not know of the terrible conditions that the men endured and there was clearly a conspiracy of silence among the officers and even among the men themselves. The soldiers on the Western Front repressed their emotions and fears in true "manly" fashion, a point of which Faulks is clearly aware. Stephen, Captain Gray, and Michael Weir are constructed by Faulks in such a way that they perform the aspects of masculinity that are required of the "soldier hero," but each deviates from the "norm" in some way and each articulates their fears in their own particular way. Gray is an unorthodox officer whose men fear him. He has "the brisk manner of the regular soldier" but this is juxtaposed with images that confer on him a more restrained, caring, and aesthetic side. He spends much of his spare time reading, he carries volumes of verse in his pocket, and his dugout always has a small shelf of books above the bed (p. 132). His reading matter also contains "some of the works of the Viennese school of psychiatrists" and he talks about "motivating and understanding" the men (p. 133). He is practically a "new" man in that respect.

Michael Weir is also a complex character. He is a figure of authority to his men, they respect him and his leadership but he also shows fear, he is superstitious and he needs constant reassurance from Stephen when they are alone together. He also admits that at the age of thirty-two he has "never . . . been with a woman."

(p. 123). Michael breaks down at one point while with Stephen in a shell hole:

"Hold me," said Weir. "Please hold me."
    He crawled over the soil and laid his head against Stephen's chest. He said, "Call me by my name."
    Stephen wrapped his arm around him and held him. "It's all right, Michael. It's all right, Michael. Hold on. Don't let go. Hold on. Hold on." (p. 192).

In this instance it is Stephen Wraysford to whom he turns and who therefore represents the required elements of strong and dependable masculinity. But, in line with his portrayal of other male characters, Faulks also problematizes Stephen's performance of masculinity elsewhere in the novel. He has many of the required elements of heroic masculinity but he is shown to have a vulnerable side when he writes that he is afraid and frightened to die alone "with no one to touch" him (p. 178). He is also aware that he has to show an example to the men and that they will look to him for reassurance. Stephen has a rational, enquiring mind, an attribute often linked to masculinity. He is "curious to know what's going to happen" and he says, "no-one in England knows what this is like. If they could see the way these men live they would not believe their eyes. This is not a war, this is an exploration of how far men can be degraded. I am deeply curious to see how much further it can be taken . . . if I didn't have that curiosity I would walk into enemy lines and let myself be killed" (p. 122). He knows that "some crime against nature is about to be committed" before the battle of the Somme but he is such a perverse character that the worse the horror is, the more he exhibits a will to survive.
    Stephen's conflict between his feelings of anger at the conditions

that he and his men experience is juxtaposed with his need to discover just how far human endeavor can go. Stephen feels he is "irrelevant" to his men and he also admits that "sometimes he thinks he despises them" (p. 125). Gray informs him that he has to make his men love him, because then "they'll fight better. And they'll feel better about it too" (p. 133). He is often described as cold and unfeeling, but he has detached himself from the horror because he needs to be an observer to survive.

The affirmation of male homosocial relationships is an important aspect of masculinity in the novel and through the relationship of Stephen and Michael, Faulks elevates this to a very high point. He also acknowledges that some men enjoy the experience of war and some actually flourish. Michael Weir joins the army to escape the narrow confines of his life in middle-class England, and in many ways it is shown to be the making of him as a man. He responds very well to those aspects of male bonding within homosocial relationships and says, "I liked the comradeship. It was as simple as that. I had no friends before, and suddenly I found that I had, if not the friendship then at least the company of hundreds of men of my age" (p. 125). The high idealism of so many male characters is interesting in Faulks's portrayal of men and Michael clearly exhibits these tendencies. For him the war is initially a great and glorious endeavor, but Faulks very carefully shows how he is affected over time by the horror and degradation that surrounds him. In one of the most descriptive and horrifying images portrayed in the novel, Michael waits in a shell hole for darkness to fall so that he can return to the trenches. As he waits (with Stephen) he sees:

The earth began to move. To their right a man who had lain still since the first attack, eased himself upright, then fell again when his damaged leg would not take his weight. Other single men moved, and began to come up like worms from their shellholes, limping, crawling, dragging themselves out. Within minutes the hillside was seething with the movement of the wounded as they attempted to get back to their line. . . .

It was like a resurrection in a cemetery twelve miles long. Bent agonized shapes loomed in multitudes on the churned earth, limping and dragging back to reclaim their life. It was as though the land were disgorging a generation of crippled sleepers, each one distinct but related to its twisted brother as they teemed up from the reluctant earth (p. 192)

This is the moment that leads to Weir's breakdown. It is not just that he did not realize there were so many men lying injured in no man's land, it is the noise that accompanies the men on their tortuous journey back to the relative safety of the trenches. It is in Faulks's descriptive narrative at this point that the real horrors are evoked: "It was a low, continuous moaning . . . the sound ran down to the river on their left and up over the hill for half a mile or more . . . it sounded . . . as if the earth itself was groaning." This is very powerful in its portrayal of the horror that leads to the breakdown of men like Michael. "Oh God oh God" he cries, "What have we done" (p. 192). At this point he turns and sobs in Stephen's arm and the strength of their friendship is evident.

The friendships between men, even love between men, is sanctioned and encouraged during war. It has to be the right kind of love though, this is always made absolutely clear. In *Dismembering the Male: Men's Bodies, Britain and the Great War*, Joanna Bourke provides a wide-ranging debate on bonding between men during the war and also recognizes that masculinity (as performative gender identity) is multi-dimensional. The relationships between men are, as she argues, extraordinarily close, almost consanguineous (related by blood). In the male world of war, "men play all the required parts: parent, sibling, friend [and] lover." However, while male bonding in war is legitimized, and the shared experiences of men in the trenches brings them into the most intimate of relationships, these close associations fail to offer any true redefinition of masculinity outside of those environments. Bourke also engages in a debate on the differences between male bonding as an "organic sentiment" of war and the fostering of a sense of group solidarity by the military authorities, stating that although:

wartime experiences may have given greater potential for experimentation in intimacy between men and may have injected a new uncertainty into romantic masculinity, [this] failed to result in any true reconstruction of masculine intimacy. (pp. 126–127)

Whereas bonding between soldiers was positively encouraged during World War I, the British national preoccupation at this time with "Sodomites" and those of a "homogenic persuasion" accentuates Bourke's point; intimacy between men was not to be condoned, apart from in the exceptional circumstance of war. The preoccupation with intimacy between soldiers is revealed in Richard Aldington's *Death of a Hero* where he remonstrates with the reader against seeing any form of homosexual desire in his writing about men. He says, "let me at once disabuse the eagle-eyed Sodomites among my readers by stating emphatically once and for all that there was nothing sodomitical in these friendships [between soldiers]." The notion that homosexual desire and practice should be invisible is questionable. According to Trudi Tate, homo-eroticism and homosexuality were present among soldiers as among any other area of society. She also states that the war provided opportunities for erotic relationships among men that were not necessarily available in peacetime. It is interesting that Faulks, unlike Pat Barker in the *Regeneration* trilogy, does not engage overtly with male erotic relationships during war.

However, the quasi-sexual elements of male friendship *are* shown in Faulks's narrative in his use of the male body, particularly the working-class male body. Working-class men are frequently connected to masculinity in its most essential form. For example, Andrew Tolson believes that, "manual labour is suffused with masculine qualities and given certain sensual overtones . . . The toughness and awkwardness of physical work and effort . . . takes on masculine lights and depths and assumes a significance beyond itself." Jack Firebrace recognizes the powerful masculinity inherent in the working man's body:

Jack stood behind Shaw, admiring his huge back, with the muscles slabbed and spread out across his shoulder blades, so that his waist, although substantial enough, looked like a nipped-in funnel by comparison . . . above the dimple of the coccyx and the fatty swell of his hair-covered buttocks. (p. 115)

There is perhaps just a glimpse of homo-eroticism in his appreciation of other man's body but that is as far as Faulks is prepared to go.

Attributes of masculinity are paramount to the idea of national identity, as Joanne Sharp also argues, stating that "men are incorporated into the nation metonymically . . . the nation is embodied within each man and each man comes to embody the nation." The war section of *Birdsong* opens with a sense of urgency and immediacy, with an image of Jack Firebrace on his back digging a tunnel. He represents all that is relevant in terms of working-class masculinity in that we are made acutely aware of the physical body at work:

Jack Firebrace lay forty-five feet underground with several hundred thousand tons of France above his face . . . His back was supported by a wooden cross, his feet against the clay, facing towards the enemy. With an adapted spade, he loosened quantities of soil into a bag which he passed back to Evans, his mate, who then crawled away in the darkness . . . He had lost track of how long he had been underground. He found it easier not to think when he might be relieved, but to keep digging. The harder he worked the easier it seemed. (p. 99)

Once again Faulks shows how important the homosocial friendships are to groups of men of the same class. Evans is his friend, his partner, and his lifeline. "Evans helped him regain his position . . . Evans swore beneath his breath and Jack reached out and gripped him in rebuke . . . They could hear the roar of their breathing magnified in the silence. They held their breath and there was nothing. They had dug to the end of the world. Jack could smell the damp earth and the sweat from Evan's body" (p. 101). The repetition of "Evans" is important in this respect and it is through these close connections between men that Faulks shows how male bonding and close physical relationships help the men through their crises and help them survive the appalling conditions in which they live.

Faulks incorporates many different male characters in the war section and there are many versions of masculinity in crisis on show. Turner, who is "a tired, frightened man" is shown "shivering with fatigue" (p. 100) and Tipper, the young soldier breaks down in the trenches:

A sharp wailing began a few yards down the trench. It was a shrill demented sound that cut through even the varying sounds of gunfire. A youth . . . ran along the duckboards, then stopped and lifted his face to the sky. He screamed again, a sound of primal fear that shook the others who heard it. His thin body was rigid and they could see the contortions of his facial muscles beneath the skin. He was screaming for his home. (p. 120).

Men such as Tipper who suffer from "male hysteria" were badly let down by both the military and medical professions. Many who returned home were considered to be degenerates and they were virtually ignored by society, but psychiatrists like W.H.R. Rivers and doctors such as Charles Myers slowly gained recognition for their work with shell shocked soldiers. It was generally acknowledged that upper-class men could break down but this was mistakenly believed to be because of the extra anxiety leadership entails. However, the plight of working-class men was looked at in a somewhat different light. If they broke down it was because they came from the "dregs of society" and were "degenerates and cowards." It seems that many also believed that lack of education contributed to the propensity of the "other ranks" to break down. According to Showalter, there were many theories put forward about the breakdown of the working-class male and these range from being "childlike" and "sulky and negative" to suffering from "latent homosexuality." It is obvious that class antagonism throws light on these diagnoses and they are also indicative of how the "other ranks" were seen. Rivers maintains that mutism was by far the most common symptom of shell shock in the "other ranks," while officers tended to stammer. The class divide is clearly recognized by Faulks in that Lieutenant Hartington has a stammer as a result of his war experiences, while after the war Stephen did not speak for three years and Brennan rarely spoke again. As "manliness" is a fundamental requisite for the military, any breakdown of a prescribed masculinity is problematic. It is easier to brand men who break down as "cowards" than it is to recognize neurasthenia or shell shock as a psychological complication. In a revealing episode in *Birdsong*, on the eve of battle officers read out the names of soldiers court-martialed (and executed) for cowardice in the face of the enemy. In this one scene Faulks gives a telling indictment of the way the army dealt with the breakdown of its soldiers.

THE WAR AND CLASS ANTAGONISM

In *Working-Class Cultures in Britain 1890–1960*, Joanna Bourke discusses the gradation of men destined to be soldiers policing the lines of the Western Front. At the time, medical inspectors graded men of the "other ranks" into four groups. Grade 1 are men who are fit, Grade 2 are "adequate" men, Grade 3 consists of men unable to walk five miles, and Grade 4 is composed of men in even worse health. From 1917 onwards just under half the recruits sent to the Western Front were deemed to be in the last two categories. Faulks shows that men such as Jack Firebrace join the army for better pay and better food and to get away from the poverty they experience at home. The miners especially join the army for a better rate of pay, a point that Faulks brings to the attention of the reader. In *Birdsong* the men are shown to be in pretty poor condition, leading one character to muse that the men in general look at least ten years older than they claim to be. Paul Fussell talks about the "*versus*" habit of the army that allows "gaping distinctions" between the officers and men and the fact that "simple antithesis [was] everywhere." This "them and us" situation is reflected throughout *Birdsong* and in the canon of World War I literature in general.

There is little doubt that the literary heritage of World War I is predominantly middle-class, and although much of the writing that came out of the conflict documented "a crisis in the life of the British nation," for many it represented the feelings of a minority class. Working-class men, for whom the war merely represented another form of capitulation to the class system, were neither writing of their own experiences or if they were they were not necessarily published. The predominant emotion that is articulated in much of the World War I literary canon is that of male, middle-class angst.

Claire Tylee points out in *The Great War and Women's Consciousness* that many officers "saw their "men" from the outside . . . [and]
presented the Tommy with affectionate contempt." At one point
when representing the view of a soldier of the horrors of Passchendaele, Fussell describes him as "a *sensitive* Other Rank" (my empha-
sis) as if that is somehow unusual and the rank-and-file soldier has
no acute mental or emotional sensibility.

It may be that in many works of literature the "other ranks" are
treated with contempt but in his depiction of working-class men in
Birdsong, Faulks is one exception to the rule. He makes a consider-
able effort to show the "other ranks" to be as diverse and made up
of dissimilar elements as the "officer class." Jack Firebrace, for
example, is a wholly believable working-class character who is a
prominent figure in many of the key themes of the novel. He is also
a multifaceted character and he is shown to have a social and moral
sensibility that emphasizes his complexity. Faulks also problematizes the whole concept of working-class "manliness" with his character by making him caring and sensitive and capable of intense
love. These attributes are unusual in many literary constructions of
working-class males and it is interesting that Faulks allows him to
predominate in the war sections of the novel. An example of this is
revealed in his love for his son, "his darling boy," and his moral
sensibility is revealed when he hears of his son's death but he will
not let it shake his faith. "His [son's] life was a beautiful thing," he
says and he will "thank God for it"(p. 168). Faulks creates a memorable protagonist in Jack Firebrace and it might be said that he is
the true "hero" of the novel in that he retains his humanity and
faith almost to the end. It is highly unusual to have such a reflective
and sensitive working-class male character and Faulks must take
credit for his portrayal. Other characters such as Douglas, Reeves,
Byrne, and Wilkinson also appear in the narrative and although
they disappear into the earth of the battlefields with just the briefest

of mention, they are important in that they represent the contribution (and decimation) of the working classes.

According to Graham Dawson, World War I was an extremely bureaucratic affair that was conducted by means of a rigidly disciplined hierarchy and highly organized division of labor designed to separate those who thought (and managed) from those who acted. Stephen is shown to be one of those who "managed," albeit in a very limited manner, but he is aware that in the eyes of society he is a "temporary gentleman." Siegfried Sassoon, who was very much part of an upper middle-class establishment before, during, and after the war says in *Memoirs of a Fox Hunting Man* that the term "temporary gentlemen" is a "disgusting phrase." Sassoon's position on the merits of class tends to confirm the absurdities of class distinction in the face of carnage and desperation. He describes meeting a fellow officer whose "shirt and tie were more yellow than khaki. And his breeches were of a bright buff tint." Sassoon is aware of this indication of someone not quite "up to scratch," as his tailor had told him, when choosing khaki shirts, "You can't have them too dark." He also describes two new officers who are greeted by the Adjutant with a "prolonged scrutiny" and "unreproducible hauteur" and the words *"Christ! who's your tailor?"* In *Birdsong* this sort of absurd incident is given credence by the reception Stephen gets when he goes to buy some shirts in London on his return from the Front:

He went to a well-stocked gentlemen's outfitter near the foot of Albemarle Street. . . . A man in a morning suit came down behind the counter.

"Good morning, sir. Can I help?"

Stephen saw the man's eyes run down him and register his uniform and rank. He also saw, beneath his formal politeness, an involuntary recoil. He wondered what it was about him that repelled the man . . . (p. 285)

Stephen is left to look at an array of shirts in different colors and materials while the attendant goes to serve "a large man, in his sixties, with an expensive overcoat and homburg hat." The salesman returns to Stephen to say:

"I don't wish to hurry you sir, but if you're not happy with our choice it would perhaps be better if you tried elsewhere."

"I was finding it difficult," [Stephen] said. His jaw felt heavy as he spoke. He realized how tired he was. "Excuse me."

"I think perhaps it would be better if-"

"You don't want me in here do you?" (pp. 285–286)

The snub to Stephen is offensive and the class antagonism inherent in this confrontation is apparent. Even in the heightened atmosphere of war, class boundaries and class restrictions still hold sway. As he walks through London, Stephen is aware of people walking around "with a sense of urgency" that has nothing to do with the war; it has become meaningless to them in their everyday lives, as has the loss of so many young men predominantly from the working classes. He buys a newspaper and notes that there is no news of the war on the front page, only details of a financial scandal and an accident in a factory. There is no acknowledgement of the lives lost or the conditions of the men in the trenches. Ironically, the only news forthcoming about the war was "a report on Fifth Army manoeuvres and warm praise for the tactical expertise of its commander" (p. 287). As the descriptive elements of the novel succinctly reflect the incompetence of command in incidents such as these, the irony of the situation is apparent, as is the absolute negation of the men of the "other ranks" and the contribution they make to the war effort.

The differences between the classes is made obvious through the narrative, and as with so much of Faulks's writing he feels no need to intrude into the narrative to pass comment. Michael Weir, for example, plays the piano for his men and "blanches with embarrassment" when they sing sentimental songs. He cannot bear to be near them during their periods of rest and relaxation and he promises himself "he would never again socialize with the other ranks" (p. 117). He does not lack compassion but like many of his class he makes no attempt to understand the reasons behind the men's conduct. It is left up to Jack Firebrace once again to be the knowing and astute observer of the real reasons for the men's behavior:

Jack noticed how men like Wheeler and Jones treat each day as if it were a shift at work and talked to one another in the evening, in the nagging joking way they would have done at home. Perhaps in some way he did not understand, that was what the two officers had been doing; perhaps all that talk about life-drawing was just a way of pretending everything was normal. (p. 116).

He at least tries to understand the officers' behavior, while Michael feels nothing but loathing for their behavior. The two men have more in common than Michael realizes as neither of them manages to become immune to the life he is living. Jack comments that each time he returns to the Front he feels "the low onset of dread" and acknowledges that "each time he seemed to have to look deeper into his reserves of mindless determination"(p. 117). At times during the novel it appears that Jack Firebrace is the only character who has a true self-knowledge and an understanding of the situation in which he finds himself. It is in the comparative characters of Weir and Firebrace that Faulks allows the class debate to surface and to show that there are no real moral and ethical differences between men in the middle and working classes. Their destinies are totally entwined in that respect, they all die and most of them die "calling for their mother."

Faulks's representation of the "other ranks" is interesting in many ways. Whereas his writing might be labeled realism and/or naturalism he makes no attempt to portray the men through "naturalistic" language. A comparison can be made here to Richard Aldington's *Death of a Hero*, which first appeared in print in 1929. It is a novel that is also written in three parts and tells the story of a young man, George Winterbourne, before, during, and up to his death in World War I. It is interesting to compare Aldington's representation of the other ranks with Faulks's representation:

"And all the time I was delirious after I was wounded I kep' seein' them aeryplanes goin' round and round and then makin' a dive at me."

" 'Struth! I got me tunic and me trowses all 'ung up in Fritzes wire, an' I couldn't get orf. Got me pockets full o' bombs, I 'ad, as well as them stick-bombs in paniers. One of the paniers was 'ung up too, an' I ses to meself, I ses, 'If you drop them fuckin' bombs, Bert, you'll blow yer fuckin' 'ead orf.' And there was old Fritz's machine-gun bullets whizzin' by, *zip, zip*. I could see 'em cuttin' the wire—and me cursin' and blindin', Blimey! I wasn't arf afraid."(*Death of a Hero*, p. 239)

Aldington, who fought in France between 1916 and 1918 both as a private and later as an officer, says the men "sometimes displayed an uncouth humour" (p. 240), and he gives plenty of examples of it in his novel. By comparison, Faulks's "men" are remarkably restrained in their language, although at one point one of the officers is moved to say that a particular soldier uses "that word" so often it ceases to be noticed. Perhaps Faulks feels that any attempt to portray the language of the men will render them comical and demeaned somehow, and that a phonological realization of the "other ranks" would be nothing better than a caricature. Only in the heat of battle does Faulks allow his men to give vent to their feelings: "the fucking Lewis gun . . . fucking eaten alive" and "all one could hear was 'Jesus' and the other 'fucking gun'" (p. 185). There is no attempt to "capture" the essence of the men's language apart from in the letters they write home. Faulks's descriptive style of writing and his attention to detail are more precisely used to portray the class differences. The representation of the men is important and as such Faulks's portrayal takes on a particular significance. Although Faulks's narrative is not so vivid or "alive" as Aldington's, he does evoke the reader's sympathies more with his restrained characterization and this is important when considering the huge number of working-class men who died.

In the Battle of the Somme in 1916, out of 110,000 men who attacked the German lines 60,000 were killed or wounded in one day, many of them in the first few hours. In *The Great War and Modern Memory*, Fussell attributes a number of causes to this tragedy, but argues that one cause "was traceable to the class system and the assumptions it sanctioned." He goes on to say:

The regulars of the British staff entertained an explicit contempt for the rapidly trained new men of "Kitchener's Army," largely recruited among workingmen from the Midlands. The planners assumed that these troops . . . were too simple and animal to cross the space between the opposing trenches in any way except in broad daylight and aligned in rows or "waves."

It was felt that more subtle tactics like rushing from cover to cover, or assault firing, or following close upon a continuous creeping barrage would confuse the troops. Faulks shows how the disdain felt for these men is revealed in the tactics the officers devised for them and he illustrates most revealingly how this contempt condemned

the men to death as they climbed out of their trenches and slowly
walked towards the lines of German machine guns:

He could see Ellis looking at his watch. He went up to him and put his
arm round his shoulders. Ellis's stricken face encouraged him; from somewhere he found a smile of reassurance to go with the squeeze he gave his
shoulders . . .
    Stephen looked up to the sky where the first light was cracking the
clouds. "Oh God, oh God," he breathed, shuddering down his spine.
Where now was the loving unity of the world?. . . . A whistle blew, and
clumsily the men began to clamber up the ladders, weighed down by their
heavy packs, into the metal air.
    Stephen watched their foolish, crab-like movements and felt his heart
seize up with pitying love for them. (pp. 300–301)

Before this moment of realization Stephen's loyalties are split between the men he commands and the officer class into which he is
educated. His previous self-willed coldness towards his men is
shown as a symptom of his determination "not to feel," but he is
shown to be broken down by the horror he is forced to undergo and
at this moment he learns to "love" his men in a way he previously
had not.

    In his depiction of the "other ranks" Faulks shows his own
"pitying love" for the thousands of "ordinary" men who died in
these deadly encounters and he is clearly not afraid to tackle the
question of class discrimination in his writing. In the narrative he
reveals how the "other ranks" are forced to exist in subhuman
conditions and how their lives are wasted for just a few yards of
territory. However, Faulks also shows them to have dignity and to
have pride in their work and their abilities. The characters have
their lives mapped out for them and we know what happens to most
of them at that specific time and in that specific place. These men

are trapped in time and space and this has a disturbing and harrowing effect on the reader as they come to know the true meaning of "cannon fodder" and the strength of class antagonism during the war. The men fight and die in their thousands for a country that did not recognize their true worth and one that will not necessarily offer them a future if and when they return.

3

The Novel's Reception

Birdsong's reception is interesting in that it was almost universally popular not only with the reading public, but also with "literary" reviewers and the popular press alike. As such it has that rare distinction of crossing the border between the "popular novel" and the "literary novel;" highly acclaimed by critics yet far outstripping the sales of other "literary" novels published at the same time. The novel's reception is also intriguing in that the format of the book is discussed almost as much as the story itself. There is little doubt, however, that Faulks's status as a writer has grown substantially since the publication of *Birdsong*, and although Stephen Moss claims that Faulks writes novels with "literary intent" but not "literary novels," he is now seen as an important contemporary writer and one who is "unsurpassed" as a writer of historical novels.

The reviews of *Birdsong* were for the most part exceptionally good. Nigel Watts describes *Birdsong* as "literature at its very best" and says that the representation of the horrors of trench warfare is told with "exquisite pathos." He is full of praise for the novel that he sees has "the power to reveal the unimagined." These sentiments are echoed by Phil Hogan, a fellow novelist and critic who argues that the novel is a "brilliant and harrowing tale of love and war" and that Faulks is a "fluent, lucid writer." The most conspicuous aspect of the novel's reception is the recognition of the power of Faulks's writing in the sections where he singles out the lives of men such as Stephen Wraysford, Michael Weir, and Jack Firebrace to accentuate the full horror of the war. Faulks says that he was hesitant about trying to capture the experience of "real" people and he felt that one way of overcoming these fears was to make sure he understood where these dreadful events happened and why they had happened. It is this sense of history and its concomitant sense of horror that most reviewers felt gave his writing such emotional strength. The dilemma that is dramatized in the war sections is one of strength in the face of absolute abjection and horror, and this is perhaps why critics find these sections of the book the most vital and absorbing and the most powerfully realized.

In newspapers, book reviews, literary journals, and magazines in places as widespread as London, New York, South Africa, Australia, and New Zealand, the critical appreciation of the novel was almost universal. *Birdsong* was hailed as one of the great British novels of the 1990s. Reviewers saw it ostensibly as a book in many guises; some argue that it is about World War I and the consequences of that war, together with memories of the war today, while others are of the opinion that it is about the power of love and the search for family. While most reviewers agreed that the book is "remarkable" in many ways, there was also a strong element of criticism in relation to the different sections of the book. There was some discord among critics as to the viability and credibility of the two sections that begin and end the novel. The main part of the narrative is seen as the story of Jack Firebrace's, Michael Weir's, and Stephen Wraysford's experiences during the war, and it is this section of the novel that held critics and reviewers in thrall. The final section set in the contemporary period was seen by some as "irrelevant," and the first section that deals with the affair between Stephen and Isabelle was criticized as having "Mills and Boon tendencies." Other critics saw this section as a powerful discourse on the overwhelming power of sexual passion. Sue Gee in the *Times* describes *Birdsong* as "a tour-de-force, engrossing, moving and unforgettable" and Kate Saunders in *The Sunday Times* states that *Birdsong* is a "remarkable attempt to unlock the experience of the first world war . . . without the political cynicism that colours most modern treatments of this catastrophe." The war sections of the novel are uniformly singled out for great praise from critics, writers, and historians alike. The accounts of combat are claimed to be among the finest that have been written, especially by a contemporary writer. They are reported as being "magnificent, deeply moving and rich in detail," and in the *Los Angeles Times* the reviewer describes them as "so powerful as to be almost unbearable." Reviewers in *The Sunday Telegraph*, *The Observer*, and *The Scotsman* describe Faulks's work as "the literary novel for the people," "a unique . . . and heart-warming novel," "a beautifully crafted novel," and "a novel to cherish and delight" respectively.

The novel is somewhat unique in uniting tabloid and broadsheet reviewers in their praise, and even more surprising is the breadth of publications in which the commendatory reviews appeared. *Today, Guardian, Observer, Daily Mail, Mail on Sunday, Sunday Express, Sunday Telegraph, TLS, TES, Spectator*, and the *Scotsman* are among those papers and supplements who gave favorable reviews to the novel. David Horspool in *The Times Literary Supplement* writes that "Faulks's preference for the simple over the bombastic helps him view the more familiar episodes in his story from a new perspective" and he argues persuasively that Faulks's picture of trench life is "meticulously presented." One critic went so far as to claim that Faulks's description of the night before the Battle of the Somme was as moving as the scene in *Henry V* before the Battle of Agincourt.

Birdsong also achieved international critical acclaim. Simon Schama, the eminent historian and writer, says in *The New Yorker* that the novel is "overpowering and beautiful" as well as "ambitious, outrageous and poignant." He goes on to say that it is "a great novel" and that "the power (of the novel) comes as much from its intensely physical realization of life, and especially sensual life, as from its evocation of death." Rob Howe writes in the influential *People Magazine* that the novel "transcends popular fiction and earns a place on a shelf with works of true literature" and argues that Faulks is a superb storyteller and a true literary craftsman. The novel was highly acclaimed in many reviews right across the United States. Leon Hale in the *Houston Chronicle* recommends the novel as one that will "pull you inside out and keep you there" and he writes that *Birdsong* allows us to understand the stupidity of the slaughter that was World War I. Harry Levins reviews *Birdsong* in the *St. Louis Post-Dispatch* and sees it as a "brooding, pessimistic work." He finds the novel "haunting" in its meditation on death and redemption and says that Faulks's painstaking detail of the everyday life of the British infantry and the enlisted British sappers, set to work tunneling beneath the German lines is "impressive."

Suzanne Ruta, a fellow writer, reviews the novel in *Newsday* and sees the book as an old-fashioned novel, "solidly plotted, vividly imagined, with a forgiving, God's-eye view of human frailty and a rhetoric to match." Ruta compares Faulks to Thomas Hardy and claims that Stephen Wraysford could almost be a character from one of Hardy's fictions. She writes that Faulks's version of the events surrounding the Battle of the Somme in 1916 is "from first to last, a very fine piece of historical writing." There are many other extremely advantageous reviews in the United States, many attesting to the "authenticity" and emotional power of the novel. Charles Flowers in *Bookpage* describes the novel as "an epic novel of love and war that radically defies conventional expectations" because of Faulks's "extraordinary gift for significant physical detail combined with his surprising characterizations." He says that *Birdsong* may have been a bestseller in England "partly because the historical background is quite literally close to home and still poignant in the national psyche," but he claims that Faulks also creates a world that should be "memorably accessible to American readers" who do not know anything about the fields of Flanders. Faulks is generally praised for his depictions of life in the trenches and in particular for his portrayal of the claustrophobic world of the underground tunnellers.

However, while the praise for the novel was prevailing and widespread, there was some dissent. Many critics felt it to be almost obligatory to discuss the format of the novel and comment upon the merits of each individual section. The consensus is that *Birdsong*, although without doubt a meritorious and commendable novel, it is not without its flaws. Susannah Herbert in the *Sunday Telegraph* feels that Faulks's writing in the first section, the love story set in pre-war France, is "dangerously close . . . to Mills and Boon" and wonders if Faulks is a secret bodice-ripper. (Interestingly, Faulks was later to be awarded the Bad Sex Award for a scene in *Charlotte Gray*.) But Herbert concludes that Faulks manages to escape any potential problems with what she sees as the weaker sections of the novel by the power of the other sections. In general, the opening section of the novel set in Amiens was well received. The first hundred pages are described by Quentin Crewe as "the most stirringly erotic" he has read for years. Even Michael Gorra, who criticizes Faulks for his portrayal of Isabelle and Stephen and claims they "never quite convince as people of 1910" says that the sex scenes, "while always decorous in language, are some of the most satisfyingly graphic" he has read. The most conspicuous criticism has been directed towards the modern day sections, which have been described as "irrelevant," "thin," and "intrusive". Michael Gorra calls the modern day sections "so lackluster that they seem a kind of injustice." While recognizing that Faulks has something to say about the fact the past can be recovered and used "to add meaning to contemporary life," Gorra feels this detracts from the "superb" section that deals with the war, especially the scenes in the tunnels. He believes the sections that deal with the concerns of Elizabeth are "extraordinarily obtuse for someone presented as both intelligent and well educated" and that for him this is what stops him from believing in any of the contemporary scenes. Kate Saunders also calls these sections "flat stuff" but argues quite persuasively that they are more than tolerable because of the way it weaves "the birdsong signature tune into the lives of subsequent generations."

There was also some dissent in the reception of Faulks's portrayal of women. Sarah Belo praises Faulks for giving equal voice to the female characters, something not normally found in novels that have war as a major theme, while others see his portrayal of women as "laughable." Although Belo thinks Faulks should be commended for giving female characters space in the novel, she also has some reservations about Elizabeth's "comfortable life," and believes Faulks slightly belittles "the unique struggles of . . . modern day existence." As with other critics, Belo believes this is a minor problem in what is otherwise a "skilful, complex novel." It appears that critics are also torn between the power of Faulks's narrative and his highly questionable use of symbolism. Charles Flowers notes that the fact the novel ends with a birth might seem too "doggedly symbolic a resolution, at first glance," but later concedes that "Faulks's compassionate dramatization and vivid description make the moment powerfully effective." Simon Schama also calls Faulks to task for his use of symbols and argues that his "penchant for avian symbols — crows, larks, canaries — that flap and twitter at significant moments of the narrative" is intensely irritating. He also concedes however, that *Birdsong* "is not a perfect novel — just a great one." Generally, reviewers agree that it is the strength of Faulks's descriptive narrative with his ability to portray the stultifying but emotionally charged atmosphere of pre-war Amiens and the horrors of life in the trenches that sets the novel apart.

4

The Novel's Performance

When *Birdsong* was published in September 1993 it achieved a popularity and breadth of readership virtually unknown for a serious novel of literary intent. It received exceptionally high praise from literary reviewers and from the reading public alike and it was seen as one of the most outstanding novels of the year. The novel was also promoted in the press as a serious contender for the 1993 Booker Prize, alongside Pat Barker's *The Eye in the Door*, Vikram Seth's *A Suitable Boy*, Carol Shields's *The Stone Diaries*, and Roddy Doyle's *Paddy Clarke Ha Ha Ha*, thereby elevating it immediately to "literary" status. Although some critics argue that the novel is "flawed," this did not diminish its popularity; in the United Kingdom alone it has sold 14,000 copies in hardback and a staggering 1.3 million copies in paperback to date. A survey by *Bookcase* also places Faulks in the top ten authors in the United Kingdom for book sales, second only to Danielle Steel, and outselling other well-known popular writers such as Maeve Binchy, Louis de Bernieres, Catherine Cookson, Nick Hornby, Tom Clancy, Wilbur Smith, and Ian McEwan.

The novel was in the bestseller lists of paperback books in the

United Kingdom for an almost unprecedented number of weeks between 1997 and 2000. It also figured prominently in many of the "best of the year" lists of 1993, culminating in a place (number eight) in the top ten books of the year based on the views of literary critics and reviewers in most of the major British broadsheet newspapers. In January 1997 a television and bookshop poll among British readers placed *Birdsong* in their top fifty books of the century, and Waterstones' readers voted the novel number forty-seven in the list of the top 100 books of the twentieth century. The novel performed so well in the bestseller lists and it was so popular with the reading public that when the BBC was looking around for a novel to launch its book discussion program, *Bookclub* on Radio 4, *Birdsong* was chosen as the first novel.

In the United States *Birdsong* featured heavily in the July 1997 bestseller compilations. Its popularity in the United States was widespread and in a poll compiled from a survey of book stores in such diverse places as East Hampton, Setauket, Bay Shore, Bellport, Huntington, and Manhattan, it was placed at number four on the best seller paperback lists, only beaten by such "popular" novelists as Ken Follett and Stephen King. *Birdsong* is also an international bestseller and has been sold in many countries, including Italy, France, Spain, Latin America, Germany, Portugal, Brazil, Denmark, Poland, Israel, Sweden, Estonia, Japan, Turkey, Bulgaria, Serbia, Finland, and Holland. It performed exceptionally well in Australia and New Zealand and it featured heavily in their bestseller and "what's hot" reading lists for a number of years. In December 2001, seven years after its publication, *Birdsong* is now perceived to be one of the "classic" literary novels of the last century and it has recently been sold as a package with two other bestselling novels. It is still selling strongly throughout the world.

Birdsong also performs exceptionally well in the list of top requests for library borrowing in the United Kingdom where it has been one of the most heavily requested contemporary novels of the last decade. It also has the distinction of uniting the New Labour Party and the Conservative Party in the United Kingdom, when both Cherie Booth (Mrs. Tony Blair) and William Hague listed it among their favorite books. Not surprisingly, given the novel's literary and historical merits, the novel is now also a prominent part of educational studies both in the United Kingdom and the United States. *Birdsong* is recognized reading on a number of World War I literature courses where it is studied alongside the war poets such as Wilfred Owen, Siegfried Sassoon, and Rupert Brooke. On many Advanced Level English Literatures GCSE courses in England the novel is required reading alongside other contemporary World War I novels such as Pat Barker's *Regeneration*, *The Eye in the Door*, and *The Ghost Road*. *Birdsong* is also making an appearance on numerous college and university courses. Amherst College and Berkeley in the United States both have the novel on their reading lists, as does Liverpool College and University of East Anglia in the United Kingdom. It also appears as suggested reading on other further and higher education literature courses and in one university in the United States it is required reading on a political science seminar in war and peace. The novel is seen to have quality and is deemed worthy of "serious" study; it is now widely accepted as a teaching tool among academics.

Faulks's novels perform so well with the reading public and they are of sufficient literary intent that they are deemed to be particularly open to cinematic adaptation. The film rights to *Birdsong* have apparently been brought by Working Title productions and at the time when Faulks gave an interview to David Rennie in 1997, the film was in pre-production. According to Nigel Reynolds, however, there are script problems that mean the film is delayed and the date of release is not yet known. The director of the film is listed as Iain Softley and the story of Stephen Wraysford in *Birdsong* follows a recognized theme in several of Softley's films. In *Backbeat* (1992), the United States film *Hackers* (1995), and in *The Wings of the Dove* (1997), Softley portrays a rites-of-passage story and a love story and *Birdsong* will make a strong addition to this *oeuvre*. The appeal of Faulks's writing lies in the strength of his characterizations and this makes then especially suitable for film. The film rights to *The Girl at the Lion d'Or* have been bought and there is, apparently, a fierce bidding war for the film rights to his latest novel, *On Green Dolphin Street*.

Sebastian Faulks's profile as a writer of literary intent has risen quite dramatically since the publication and success of *Birdsong*. He is now listed in the latest edition of *The Oxford Companion to English Literature* and he has been nominated for a number of literary prizes and awards. He was nominated for the Securicor Omega Express Author of the Year in 1994 and for the Author of the Year in the British Book Awards of 1995. In 1996 Faulks was among the contenders on the long list for the IMPAC Dublin Literary Award and in 1998 he was nominated for the highly prestigious James Tait Black Memorial Award for *Charlotte Gray*.

5

Further Reading and Discussion Questions

This chapter provides topics and proposals for further discussion together with suggested further reading of novels with similar themes and preoccupations. It also provides a short selected criticism (literary and historical) that foregrounds some of the issues raised by the questions. There are also details of a number of websites that cover World War I literature, historical sites, and more general sites that have discussions of either Sebastian Faulks's writing or discussions of contemporary fiction. Additionally, there are sites that offer recommendations and guidance in how to set up your own reading club or discussion group. There are other sites that can be found by following the links on those detailed here, but those listed have been found to be the most useful and/or the most interesting.

The questions suggested for discussion range across a number of issues and many different levels of engagement, some of which are introduced in Section 2. They offer the chance to discuss the broader sweeps of *Birdsong* and some of the more specialized and challenging aspects of the novel. There are also questions that draw

upon more critical and theoretical aspects of contemporary literature.

DISCUSSION QUESTIONS

1. Stephen Wraysford is a character full of contradictions. Faulks
   wanted him to be "compelling," but he is lonely and brooding
   and is described as a "cold-hearted devil." How far has Faulks's
   vision of Wraysford as a compelling character been realized?
   How do other characters see him? How does he see himself at
   various times? How does he change throughout the novel?

2. Faulks says that the novel has six main characters, three male
   and three female. This presupposes that he has given equal
   weight to the representation of both sexes. Is that the case? Who
   do you see as the main protagonists in the novel? Is there any
   way this is a novel of empowerment for women? How effective
   is the characterization of Isabelle, Jeanne, and Elizabeth in
   comparison with the men? What is commendable in his representation of the women, what is problematic? Does Faulks have
   an idealistic view of women? You might look at the description
   of Françoise in relation to this idea and the descriptions of
   Isabelle and Jeanne. Look specifically at the way femininity is
   constructed. What differences, if any, can be found in the
   contemporary section and the representation of Elizabeth?

3. *Birdsong* is written in such a way that the three main sections
   intersect and inform each other. What do you think are the
   main themes of the book and how are these addressed in each
   of the sections? What effect does the fragmentation of the narrative have on the reader? How does the narrative strategy of

shifts in time and location inform and assist or hinder our reading?

4. Faulks has said that *Birdsong* is not a war story, it is a love story. If the book is a love story, who is the love interest? Is it Isabelle, Jeanne, or even Michael Weir? Is there a layering of love stories here — Stephen Wraysford's and Sebastian Faulks? You might think about the love Faulks feels for all those men who fought, and those who died Is it a love story dedicated to Britain's lost and damaged sons? Try to offer textual evidence for any of these options.

5. Discuss the different genres, such as "Romance," "Historical Novel," and "War Story" that could categorize the novel. What significance does this have to our expectations of the novel and should we try to resist such categorizations?

6. Discuss Azaire's conduct towards his wife, his children, and his workers. You might look at the relationship between the Azaires and the Bérands and the aftermath of the supper party on pages 9–14, the confrontation between Azaire and his workers on page 17 and the outing to the water gardens on pages 36–39. How do these incidents foreshadow the war sections of the novel?

7. In the cathedral at Amiens, Stephen sees a picture in his mind of a "terrible piling up of the dead," row upon row of men in the hollowed out earth. It appears that Stephen's knowledge of the future is obtained from a divine source and that he has personal insight into what is to come. Isabelle is also shown contemplating her relationship in a church and decides to leave Stephen in order to "save her soul." What significance does faith have in the novel? You might look at Stephen and Isabelle in relation to this question, but also look at the later sections with the men in the trenches and Michael Weir. How does

superstition parallel and emulate religious belief? What is it about Stephen that allows him to hold himself together under the extreme pressure of his life in the trenches? Has it to do with faith or even loss of faith?

8. Why does Isabelle leave Stephen? Why does she not tell him about her pregnancy? She says she has stopped "haemorrhaging her life away" and "the power she felt as a woman was turned inward, creating new life." What is your response to this? What does she withhold from Stephen by denying him knowledge about his daughter, especially during the war when he seeks her out?

9. What is the relevance of the color red throughout the novel? Isabelle cannot reconcile the fact that "the colour of her own blood that promised new life and liberation should manifest itself in the colour of pain." Isabelle and Stephen also make love in the red room. What literary parallels are there to the red room? What does the red room symbolize and what other meanings are attached to the color in the novel?

10. Discuss the representation of masculinity in pre-war France, during the war sections and in the contemporary setting. Does the notion of masculinity mean different things at different times? You might like to think about the notion of heroic masculinity, homosocial relationships, and the love between men during war. You should also think about the "minor" characters such as Lucien Lebrun, Bérand, Levi, Hunt, Byrne, and Robert as well as Stephen, Michael, and Jack. Compare and contrast the relationships between Stephen and Michael and Jack Firebrace and Arthur Shaw. Why are the friendships/ relationships important to the men and to the novel? What aspects of connectedness are found in these male homosocial relationships?

11. Sometimes the "voices" of the men in the trenches and tunnels
    are distinct, but more often they blend, melt into each other.
    Faulks is describing an entire world in chaos through the cen-
    tral discerning consciousness of Stephen Wraysford and sug-
    gesting how external devastation and internal fragmentation
    interact. But, it is always Stephen's story, even when he is
    absent. Have the voices and therefore the histories of the other
    men become subsumed by Stephen's narrative? Is the literary
    representation of the First World War doomed to be forever
    middle-class?

12. "Since Weir died I have not been very close to reality. I am in
    a wilderness beyond fear. Time has finally collapsed for me".
    Discuss the effects of Weir's death on Stephen. How and why
    does it change him? How does Elizabeth respond to the extract
    from Stephen's diary that details his feelings? How important is
    Stephen's diary to the making of memory—memory about the
    war and memories of her family? Think about Elizabeth's visit
    to France and to Brennan in the nursing home. Why is she
    trying to piece together the past in this way? Is Elizabeth's
    ignorance of history, even the history of her own family, indic-
    ative of the unawareness of her generation about the events of
    the past?

13. How important is the contemporary setting to the novel? Is it
    merely a literary device that enables us to "see" the horror
    through contemporary eyes? You might like to think why
    Faulks decided to include those sections. The circularity of the
    novel is obvious and the birth of Elizabeth's child links quite
    specifically to the deaths in the trenches. Is it necessary to end
    on such a note? If the ending were different, if we were not
    presented with a reaffirmation of life, what effect would this

have on the reader? How would you like to see the book end or at what point would you have stoped the narrative?

14. "No child or future generation will ever know what this was like. They will never understand. When it is over we will go quietly among the living and we will not tell them. We will talk and sleep and go about our business like human beings. We will seal what we have seen in the silence of our hearts and no words will reach us." How do you respond to Stephen's words? Do you think no future generation, or indeed, anyone who did not experience the horrors of the war will ever understand what it was like? How does *Birdsong* help or hinder that understanding?

15. What effect do Faulks's "letters home" have on the reader? You might compare the style and tone of Michael Weir's letter to his parents with that of Tipper's to his parents. Is one any less emotional than the other is despite the way they are written? Stephen writes to Isabelle, Jack Firebrace writes to his wife and Byrne writes to his brother. How do the letters correspond with the reality experienced by the men?

EDUCATIONAL RESOURCES

For historical background and war documentation contact The Imperial War Museum, Lambeth Road, London SE1 6HZ. It has a range of educational resources including documents, videos, posters, postcards, slide packs, and audio and videocassettes. These can be ordered from The Imperial War Museum, Mail Order Department, Duxford, Cambs CB2 4QR, England.

There is an organization that arranges tours of World War I battlefields: Somme Battlefield Tours, 19, Old Road, Wimbourne,

Dorset, BH211EJ, England. Telephone 01202 840520 Fax 01202 840520.

Tours of the Water Gardens in Amiens can be arranged through Les Hortillonages, 54 Boulevard Beauville, 80000-Amiens, France. Telephone 0033 322921218. This information is available from BBC *Omnibus* Factsheet at *http;//www.bbc.co.uk/factsheets/ omnibus.*

WEBSITES

http://info.ox.ac.uk

This is an exceptionally good, award winning academic site that provides virtual seminars for World War I literature. It also contains excellent links to other areas of discussion such as war poetry, and *The Hydra*, which is the magazine produced at Craiglockhart Hospital in Edinburgh, where W.H.R. Rivers treated officers suffering from shell shock, including Siegfried Sassoon and Wilfred Owen. There are also other links to follow to the British Legion, diaries and memoirs of World War I, picture archives and other major war resources. It also links to World War I Associations.

http://www.napier.ac.uk

Edinburgh's Napier University web page with leads to Craiglockhart Hospital and World War I poets.

http://news.bbc.co.uk/his/english

This is a useful site that offers an historical insight into the battles of the World War I. It also has other links to follow.

http://www.lib.byu/~rdh/wwwi

A site that provides access to document archives containing first-hand accounts of World War I.

Other useful historical and academic web sites:

http://www.FirstWorldWar.org

http://www.worldwar1.com

http://www.spartacus.schoolnet.co.uk

http://www.pitt.edu/~pugachev/greatwar/ww1.html.

http://pages.about.com/warsites/index.html (This contains memorials to the dead of WW1)

http://www.sassoonery.demon.co.uk (Dedicated to Siegfried Sassoon)

http://www.art-www1.com/gb/visite.html (Guided tour of the art of World War I)

http://www.greatwar.org/PoetsandProse/index.htm (World War I prose and poetry)

http://www.www1-propaganda-cards.com/ (Propaganda Postcards of World War I)

Reading Group web sites

http://www.readinggroupchoices.com
This site contains helpful advice on how to set up a reading group. There is a short review of *Birdsong* that is a good point to start a discussion group.

http://www.randomhouse.com/vintage/read/birdsong
This has an excellent set of questions to promote discussion of the novel.

http://www.washingtonpost.com
Follow the links to the book discussion site for an excellent forum for contemporary fiction.

http://geocities.com/SoHo/Nook/1082/Sebastian faulks page.html
This contains information about Sebastian Faulks and related novels.

http://charlottegraymovie.warnerbros.com/cmp/main.html
The official *Charlotte Gray* film web site.

FURTHER READING

Suggested further reading of works by Sebastian Faulks

A *Trick of the Light* (1984)
The Girl at the Lion D'Or (1989)
A *Fool's Alphabet* (1992)
The Fatal Englishman (1996)
The Last Enemy (with Richard Hillary, 1997)
Vintage Book of War Stories (with Jorg Hensgen,1998)
Charlotte Gray (1999)
On Green Dolphin Street (2001)

Suggested further reading of other First World War literature

Richard Aldington, *Death of a Hero*
Pat Barker, *Regeneration, The Eye in the Door, The Ghost Road,* and
    Another World
Ford Madox Ford, *The Good Soldier* and *Parade's End*
Robert Graves, *Goodbye to All That*
Susan Hill, *Strange Meeting*
Sebastien Japrisot, A *Very Long Engagement* (Translated by Linda Coverdale)
Erich Maria Remarque, *All Quiet on the Western Front*
Siegfried Sassoon, *Memoirs of an Infantry Man* and *Memoirs of a Fox-Hunting Man*

Evelyn Waugh, The Sword of Honour Trilogy: *Men at Arms, Officers and Gentlemen*, and *The End of the Battle*
Rebecca West, *The Return of the Soldier*
Virginia Woolf, *Mrs. Dalloway*

Literary criticism and theory

Bakhtin M. "The *Bildungsroman* and Its Significance in the History of Realism (Towards a Historical Typology of the Novel)," Caryl Emerson and Michael Holquist eds. *Speech Genres & Other Late Essays*, translated by Vern W. McGee. Austin: University of Texas Press, 1986.

Connell, R.W. *Masculinities*. Cambridge: Polity Press, 1995.

Connor, Steven. *Postmodernist Culture: An introduction to theories of the contemporary*. Oxford: Blackwell, 1997.

Docherty, Thomas. *Alterities: Criticism, history, representation*. Oxford: Clarendon Press, 1996.

Gasiorek, A. *Post-War British Fiction — Realism and After*. London: Edward Arnold, 1995.

Harris, G. "Compulsory Masculinity, Britain and the Great War: The literary historical work of Pat Barker." *Critique: Studies in Contemporary Fiction*. Vol. 39, June 22, 1998.

Holton, Robert. *Jarring Witnesses: Modern fiction and the representation of history*. New York & London : Harvester Wheatsheaf, 1994.

Lyotard, Jean François. *The Postmodern Condition : A Report on knowledge*. Translated by Geoff Bennington and Brian Massumi, foreword by Fredric Jameson. Manchester: Manchester University Press, 1984.

McHale, Brian. *Postmodernist Fiction*. New York ; London : Methuen, 1987.

Roper, M. and Tosh, J. Eds. *Manful Assertions: Masculinities in Britain Since 1800*. London and New York: Routledge, 1991.

Taylor, D.J. *After the War: The Novel and England Since 1945*. London: Chatto and Windus Ltd, 1993.

Thomas, C. *Male Matters: Masculinity, Anxiety and the Male Body on the Line*. Urbana and Chicago: University of Illinois Press, 1996.

Selected Bibliography

Ashworth Tony. *Trench Warfare 1914–1918: The Live and Let Live System.* New York: Holmes and Meier Publishers, Inc., 1980.

Barrie, Alexander. *War Underground.* London: W.H. Allen & Co. Ltd. 1981.

Berger, M. Wallis B. and Watson, S. Eds. *Constructing Masculinity.* New York: Routledge, 1996.

Bourke, J. *Working-Class Cultures in Britain 1890–1960: Gender, Class and Ethnicity.* London and New York: Routledge, 1994.

——— *Dismembering the Male: Men's Bodies and the Great War.* London: Reaktion Books Ltd, 1996.

Breely, S. 'Not Faulking About', *Varsity*, http://www.varsity.cam.ac.uk.

de Lisle, T. 'Too Good to be True', *Sunday Telegraph Magazine*, April 14, 1966.

Dawson, Graham. *Soldier Heroes: British Adventure, Empire and the Imagining of Masculinities.* London and New York: Routledge, 1994.

Ferro, Marc. *The Great War 1914–1918.* Routledge.

Fussell, Paul. *The Great War and Modern Memory.* London, Oxford and New York: Oxford University Press, 1975.

Gilbert, S. and Gubar, S. *No Man's Land: Volume 1, The War of the Words.* Yale University Press, 1988.

Graham, E. & Hoover, C. *Sebastian Faulks Interview*, http://www.chronicle.duke.edu

Hanley, Lynne. *Writing War: Fiction, Gender and Memory.* Amherst: The University of Massachusetts Press, 1991.

Hattenstone, S. 'In Love and War', *Guardian*, April 23, 2001.

Keegan, John. *The Face of Battle*, London: Cape, 1976.

——— *The First World War*, London: Hutchinson, 1998.

MacDonald, Lyn. *1914.* London: Penguin, 1989.

——— *Somme.* London: Michael Joseph Ltd. 1983.

——— *They Called it Passchendaele.* London: Michael Joseph, 1978.

Moss, S. 'The Old Guard', *Guardian*, G2, August 6, 2001.

Rennie, D. *Daily Telegraph*, August 18, 1997.

Ridgway, C. 'Introduction', in Richard Aldington, *Death of a Hero*. London: The Hogarth Press, 1984.

Sharp, J. 'Gendering Nationhood: A feminist engagement with national identity', in Duncan, N. ed. *Body Space*. London: Routledge, 1996.

Showalter, E. 'Male Hysteria: W.H.R. Rivers and the Lessons of Shell Shock', in *The Female Malady: Women, Madness and English Culture*. London: Virago, 1987.

—— *Hystories: Hysterical Epidemics and Modern Media*. New York: Columbia University Press, 1997.

Tate, T. *Modernism, history and the First World War*. Manchester and New York: Manchester University Press, 1998.

Tolson, A. *The Limits of Masculinity*. London: Tavistock Press, 1977.

Tylee, C.M. *The Great War and Women's Consciousness*. London: MacMillan Press, 1990.

Whitehead, A. 'Open to Suggestion: Hypnosis and History in Pat Barker's Regeneration', *Modern Fiction Studies*, Vol. 44.3, Fall, 1998.

Reviews of *Birdsong*:

Barker, E. *Independent on Sunday*, September 19, 1993

Beevor, T. *Daily Telegraph*, August 22, 1998

Cameron, E. *European*, October 14, 1993

Crewe, Q. *Daily Mail*, September 30, 1993

Dumas, A. *Denver Rocky Mountain News*, February 21, 1999

Dyer, G. *Independent*, September 20, 1993

Flowers, C. *Bookpage*

Ford, L. *Toronto Weekly Arts Newspaper*, August 29, 1996

Gee, S. *Times*, September 9, 1993

Gorra, M. *New York Times Book Review*, February 22, 1996

Hale, L. *Houston Chronicle*, June 25, 2001

Herbert, S. *Sunday Telegraph*, September 12, 1993

Hicklin, A. *Scotland on Sunday*, November 28, 1993

Hogan, P. *Observer*, September 19, 1993

Horspool, D. *Times Literary Supplement*, September 1993

Howe, R. *People Magazine*, May 6, 1996

James, A. *Sunday Express*, September 19, 1993

Levins, H. *Arizona Republic*, March 14, 1999

Lewis, P. *Mail on Sunday*, September 19, 1993

Morris, T. *Guardian*, October 19, 1993

Ruta, S. *Newsday*, February 11, 1996

Saunders, K. *Sunday Times*, September 19, 1993

Schama, S. *New Yorker*, April 1, 1996

Spalding, F. *Times Educational Supplement*, November 5, 1993

Watts, N. *Time Out* September 15–22, 1993

Yardley, J. *Washington Post Book World*, April 1996

The Bookseller, August 13, 1993

The Bookseller, August 27, 1993

Today, September 16, 1993

Notes

1. Personal information provided by Vintage publicity. Other information is taken from various interviews given by Sebastian Faulks and from Sebastian Faulks, *Book Club*, BBC Radio 4, Sebastian Faulks "The Fatal Century," *Omnibus*, BBC TV, Transmitted 24 March 2001, and Sarah Brealey, "Not Faulking Around," *Varsity*, *http://www.varsity.cam.ac.uk*. Tim de Lisle's informative interview with Faulks is also a source of information. See Tim de Lisle, "Too good to be true," *Sunday Telegraph Magazine*, 14 April 1996, pp. 14–16 and Simon Hattenstone, "In Love and War," *Guardian*, 23 April, 2001.

2. "The Fatal Century," *Omnibus*, BBC, Transmitted 24 March 2001.

3. See Sebastian Faulks, "The Wolfendens," *Observer Review*, 27 April, 1997, for a brief discussion of the background to the Wolfenden Report. See also Sebastian Faulks, "The Lost Boys," *The Times Magazine*, 13 April, 1996, pp. 16–18.

4. Sebastian Faulks, "The Lost Boys," *Times Magazine*, 13 April, 1996.

5. Sebastian Faulks, "Back to the Front with Tommy," *Guardian*, 5 September 1993. See also Sebastian Faulks, "Wot I Wrote," *Cover Magazine*, December 1997.